I0822763

THE RAIDERS AND WRITERS OF CERVANTES' ARCHIVE

The Raiders and Writers of Cervantes' Archive

Borges, Puig, and García Márquez

PAUL KONG
City University of Hong Kong, People's Republic of China

LONDON AND NEW YORK

First published 2009 by Ashgate Publishing

Published 2016 by Routledge
2 Park Square, Milton Park, Abingdon, Oxon OX14 4RN
711 Third Avenue, New York, NY 10017, USA

Routledge is an imprint of the Taylor & Francis Group, an informa business

Copyright © Paul Kong 2009

Paul Kong has asserted his moral right under the Copyright, Designs and Patents Act, 1988, to be identified as the author of this work.

All rights reserved. No part of this book may be reprinted or reproduced or utilised in any form or by any electronic, mechanical, or other means, now known or hereafter invented, including photocopying and recording, or in any information storage or retrieval system, without permission in writing from the publishers.

Notice:
Product or corporate names may be trademarks or registered trademarks, and are used only for identification and explanation without intent to infringe.

British Library Cataloguing in Publication Data
Kong, Paul
The raiders and writers of Cervantes' archive: Borges, Puig, and García Márquez
1. Cervantes Saavedra, Miguel de, 1547–1616 – Influence 2. Borges, Jorge Luis, 1899–1986 – Criticism and interpretation 3. Puig, Manuel – Criticism and interpretation 4. García Márquez, Gabriel, 1928– – Criticism and interpretation
I. Title
863.6

Library of Congress Cataloging-in-Publication Data
Kong, Paul.
The raiders and writers of Cervantes' archive: Borges, Puig, and García Márquez / by Paul Kong.
p. cm.
Includes bibliographical references.
ISBN 978-0-7546-6533-5 (alk. paper)
1. Latin American literature—Spanish influences. 2. Cervantes Saavedra, Miguel de, 1547–1616—Influence. 3. Cervantes Saavedra, Miguel de, 1547–1616—Archives. 4. Literature, Comparative—Latin American and Spanish. 5. Literature, Comparative—Spanish and Latin American. 6. Archives in literature. 7. Manuscripts in literature. 8. Borges, Jorge Luis, 1899–1986—Criticism and interpretation. 9. Puig, Manuel—Criticism and interpretation. 10. García Márquez, Gabriel, 1928—Criticism and interpretation. I. Title.

PQ7081.K66 2009
860.9'98—dc22

2008050241

ISBN 13: 978-0-7546-6533-5 (hbk)

Contents

PART 1

Archives Versus Manuscripts

Chapter 1
Exploring the Archive

> Archives keep the secrets of the state; novels keep the secrets of culture, and the secret of these secrets.
>
> González Echevarría[1]

> [T]he archive of a society, a culture, or a civilization cannot be described exhaustively; or even, no doubt, the archive of a whole period. On the other hand, it is not possible for us to describe our own archive, since it is from within these rules that we speak, since it is that which gives to what we can say – and to itself, the object of our discourse – its modes of appearance.
>
> Foucault[2]

> For the absolute memory of God, the future is always already given. We can thus conceive, for the temporal condition, an upper limit determined by a perfect recording or archival capacity. As consummate archivist, God is outside time, and this is one of the grounds of modern Western metaphysics.
>
> Lyotard[3]

In recent years, the archive, both as an establishment and as a concept, has been capturing the attention of many scholars across different disciplines, ranging from anthropology, geography, philosophy, history, sociology, literature to information science.[4] The archive is not only about the forbidden space for hoarding manuscripts or the accumulation of information. It is also about the past, about history, about how information was and can be categorized and hence manipulated, and on a

---

1 Roberto González Echevarría, *Myth and archive: A Theory of Latin American Narrative* (Durham and London: Duke University Press, 1998), p. 33.

2 Michel Foucault, *The Archaeology of Knowledge and The Discourse on Language*, trans. A.M. Sheridan Smith (New York: Pantheon Books, 1972) (Original French title: *L'Archéologie du savoir* (Paris: Gallimard, 1969)), p. 130.

3 Jean-François Lyotard, *The Inhuman: Reflections on Time* (Palo Alto, CA: Stanford University Press, 1991) (Original French title: *L'Inhumain: Causeries sur le temps*), p. 60.

4 Besides works by Jacques Derrida, Michel Foucault and Roberto González Echevarría, there have been a large number of intellectual works on the archive, for example, two special issues of the journal *History of the Human Sciences* (November 1998, Vol. 11, Issue 4 and May 1999, Vol. 12, Issue 2) as well as one issue of *Studies in the Literary Imagination* (Spring 1999; 32, 1). The importance of the concept of the archive can be revealed through the different terms used for classifying and describing different archives, like 'social archive', 'raw archive', 'imperial archive', 'postcolonial archive', 'ethnographic archive', 'geographical archive', 'liberal archive', 'archive cancer' and 'archival consciousness'. For further details on this, see Marlene Manoff's 'Theories of the Archive from Across the Disciplines', in *Portal: Libraries and the Academy*, Vol. 4, No. 1 (2004), pp. 9–25.

national level, about cultural and social manoeuvres, especially with the possibility of constructing a 'reality' at the service of ideology. At the same time, this implies the possibility of revealing the workings of ideology by knowing how knowledge is conditioned in such a 'reality' and how such a system of thought is formulated within the archive.

González Echevarría remarks that the archive has the following characteristics: '(1) the presence not only of history but of previous mediating elements through which it was narrated, be it the legal documents of colonial times or the scientific ones of the nineteenth century; (2) the existence of an inner historian who reads the texts, interprets and writes them; and finally (3) the presence of an unfinished manuscript that the inner historian is trying to complete' (1998, 22). This greatly differs from the dictionary definition of the archive: 'a place in which public records or other important historic documents are kept' (*OED*). González Echevarría looks at the archive from three perspectives: what it houses, who is authorized to access it and its manuscripts and the kind of history narrated by the archive. What it houses are unfinished manuscripts, which are the ciphers to be solved, because of which the archive is shrouded with mystery and unintelligibility. Such mystery and unintelligibility of the archive are dealt with, according to González Echevarría, by an historian, who will read, interpret and 'write' the texts, resulting in a kind of history which is mediating in nature. The importance of this history with mediating elements can be seen from the order of these three characteristics: history – historian – unfinished manuscript. It is obvious that what Echevarría foregrounds are the historical implications and dimensions of the archive.

But the concept of the archive is more complex than simply being a place for hoarding unfinished manuscripts, data and old files of the past history. This complex notion will be unpacked through the works and ideas of González Echevarría, Foucault and Derrida. González Echevarría in *Myth and Archive* looks at the Latin American 'narrative tradition' as generated by 'three manifestations of Western hegemonic discourse': the law in the colonial period, science in the nineteenth century and anthropology in the twentieth century (González Echevarría 1998, 172), and claims that the archive is inseparable from origin, secrecy and law on the cultural side and from the origin of the novel on the literary side (González Echevarría 1998, 30 and 33); Foucault focuses on the ideological centralization and homogenisation of the archive; while Derrida explores its evil, apocalyptic violence and traumatic destruction. The focus of this chapter will be along these lines. However, one way to unveil the complexity of the archive is through Wordsworth's reading and rewriting of Don Quixote in *The Prelude* Book Five in terms of apocalyptic destruction and utopian preservation.

1.1. Wordsworth: Arabian Quixote

Wordsworth's reading of Cervantes' *Don Quixote* is highly relevant to the concept of the archive in many respects. In this autobiographical text, Wordsworth enters Cervantes' archive of *Don Quixote* by inhabiting the memory of Cervantes. Wordsworth's reading of *Don Quixote* is set in a dream, and in this dream,

Don Quixote is turned into a lonely Arab, riding not a horse, but a dromedary (1850, Book 5, I. 76). Sancho Panza no longer stays with this Arabian knight. Not only is Don Quixote's identity changed, the dreamer's identity is also problematized. In the 1805 edition of *The Prelude*, it is his friend who is the dreamer, but in the 1850 edition, it is 'I' the narrator who dreams:

> While he was sitting in a rocky cave
> By the seaside, perusing as it chanced,
> The famous history of the errant knight
> Recorded by Cervantes, …
> …
> He mused – upon these chiefly – and at length,
> His senses yielding to the sultry air,
> Sleep seized him and he passed into a dream.
> He saw before him an Arabian waste,
> A desart, and he fancied that himself
> Was sitting there in the wide wilderness
> Alone upon the sands. …
> (1805, Book 5, ll. 58–74)

> While I was seated in a rocky cave
> By the sea-side, perusing, so it chanced,
> The famous history of the errant knight
> Recorded by Cervantes, …
> …
> I mused, upon these chiefly: and at length,
> My senses yielding to the sultry air,
> Sleep seized me, and I passed into a dream.
> I saw before me stretched a boundless plain
> Of sandy wilderness, …
> (1850, Book 5, ll. 58–72)

It is never sure who is actually reading Cervantes' *Don Quixote* and who is dreaming in Wordsworth's texts. In the 1805 edition, the narrator describes his memory of his friend reading *Don Quixote*, but in the 1850 edition, his memory of his friend becomes the memory of his own self. It may be that his friend is Wordsworth's own double and hence the 'I – He' distinction collapses. If the power of narrative not only draws the reader into the text, but also transforms him into its character, this transformation is complicated here. In the 1805 edition, it is Wordsworth's friend who is turned into the figure of Don Quixote but it is Wordsworth himself who is the figure of Don Quixote in the 1850 edition.

This complexity between reading, writing and identification could be unpacked through Derrida's idea of memory inhabitation and Lyotard's concept of disappropriation of consciousness. Derrida suggests that reading can be regarded as a process of inhabiting the memory of the author, when he comments on two 'greatnesses' of Joyce, especially with reference to the two words 'he war' Joyce uses in *Finnegans Wake* (258):

> Coming here, I said to myself that there are perhaps only two manners, or rather two greatnesses, in this madness of writing by which whoever writes effaces himself, leaving, only to abandon it, the archive of his own effacement. ... There is first of all the greatness of s/he who writes in order to give, in giving, and therefore in order to give to forget the gift and the given, what is given and the act of giving, which is the only way of giving, the only possible – and impossible – way. ... As for the other greatness ... *being in memory of him*. You're not only overcome by him, whether you know it or not, but obliged by him, and constrained to measure yourself against this overcoming. Being *in memory of him*: not necessarily to remember him, no, but to be in his memory, to inhabit his memory ...[5] (original italics)

For Derrida, writing means a process of self-effacement, resulting in an archive of the author's own effacement. Paradoxically, writing is also an act of giving, while reading is a process of inhabiting the author's memory. The idea of being in the memory of the author, inhabiting his memory can be more easily grasped through Lyotard's notions of time present and time past. Lyotard dissects the complexity of the notion of 'present' by tracing how a 'presenting present' becomes a present which is 'then presenting and now presented'. Any sentence, according to Lyotard, takes place in a certain temporality (that is, a 'presenting present', a 'now'). But the sentence, for example, sentence 1, could be taken as referent of another sentence, for example, sentence 2, which could say 'sentence 1 took place on the 24th June', in which sentence 1 is situated in a network of 'objective' time constituted by calendar and clock. It is also possible that sentence 1 is taken as referent of another sentence, for example, sentence 3, which is without any use of dates and hours when referring to it: 'sentence 1 was uttered yesterday'. Hence, the 'presenting present' is displaced and turned into a 'presented present' (that is, the past) (Lyotard 1991, 58–9). In other words, referencing, whether in the form of writing or memory, is always a process of temporalization of the referent of the presenting present into a presented present, and such temporalization can also be termed 'disappropriation'.

In Lyotard's view, the 'presenting present' (that is, 'now') is always a disappropriation of consciousness:

> As an occurrence, each sentence is a 'now'. It presents, now, a meaning, a referent, a sender and an addressee. With respect to presentation, we must imagine the time of an occurrence as – and only as – present. This present cannot be grasped as such, it is absolute. It cannot be synthesized *directly* with other presents. The other presents with which it can be placed in relation are necessarily and immediately changed into presented presents, i.e. past. ... Because it is absolute, the present cannot be grasped: it is *not yet* or *no longer* present. It is always too soon or too late to grasp presentation itself and present it. Such is the specific and paradoxical constitution of the event. That something happens, the occurrence,

[5] Derrida, 'Two words for Joyce' in *Post-structuralist Joyce: Essays from the French*, ed. Derek Attridge and Daniel Ferrer (Cambridge: Cambridge University Press, 1984), pp. 146–7.

> means that the mind is disappropriated. The expression 'it happens that ...' is the formula of non-mastery of self over self. The event makes the self incapable of taking possession and control of what it is. It testifies that the self is essentially passible to a recurrent alterity. (1991, 59) (original italics)

The non-synthesizable nature of the 'presenting present' changes other presents into 'presented presents', which are the 'past'. Lyotard explains that this is mainly because of the deictic nature of time, especially in the terms like 'now', 'yesterday' and 'future' (58). This 'presenting present' is not graspable because it is 'not yet' and 'no longer' present, and because of this, the mind is disappropriated, failing in making sense and taking control of the 'presenting present'. Instead, this disappropriated consciousness is comparable to memories in that both allow diversity of moments and actualization of time whenever needed. Lyotard remarks that '[b]y opposing discontinuity with synthesis, consciousness seems to be the very thing that throws down a challenge to alterity. In this conflict, what is at stake is to determine the limits within which consciousness is capable of embracing a diversity of moments and of actualizing them "each time" they are needed' (60). This consciousness which is capable of embracing a diversity of moments is what Derrida means by being in the memory of the author, by inhabiting the author's memory. This is a disappropriated consciousness which allows a diversity of moments in terms of memory.

If so, reading is a moment of creating disappropriated consciousness through which the reader will be in the author's memory, 'to inhabit his memory', which is always a memory of alterity, the other's memory. In other words, it is the power of narrative to retain and preserve the author's memory and the memory of the others through consciousness disappropriation. In this light, the text is the author's archive for disappropriated consciousness. To inhabit the author's memory is thus a homogenizing act, an act by which the reader's consciousness is disappropriated. It is an act of the reader's willing submission to the inhabitation of the author's memory, through which, the reader's consciousness is homogenized in such an archive. But the two different readers of *Don Quixote* in Wordsworth's texts show that when reading is an activity allowing the reader to inhabit the memory of the author, there is always a sense of alterity, otherness. No matter whether it is Wordsworth himself or it is his friend who inhabits Cervantes' memory, it is possible that Cervantes likewise inhabits somebody's memory while writing and reading his own text. It is for sure an important area to explore the extent of the Arabian influence on Cervantes and on his *Don Quixote*, but the importance of the Arab historian Cide Hamete Benengeli in *Don Quixote* is beyond doubt, as in Part 1, Chapter 9, the narrator discovers by chance in Toledo the manuscript of another *Don Quixote* about Don Quixote's life and adventures written by this alleged Arabian writer:

> One day when I was in the Alcaná market in Toledo, a boy came by to sell some notebooks and old papers to a silk merchant; as I am very fond of reading, even torn papers in the streets, I was moved by my natural inclinations to pick up one of the volumes the boy was selling, and I saw that it was written in characters I

> knew to be Arabic. And since I recognized but could not read it, I looked around to see if some Morisco who knew Castilian, and could read it for me, was in the vicinity, and it was not very difficult to find this kind of interpreter, for even if I had sought a speaker of a better and older language, I would have found him. In short, fortune provided me with one, and when I told him what I wanted and placed the book in his hands, he opened it in the middle, read for a short while, and began to laugh.
>
> I asked him why he was laughing, and he replied that it was because of something written in the margin of the book as an annotation. I told him to tell me what it was, and he, still laughing, said:
>
> "As I have said, here in the margin is written: 'This Dulcinea of Toboso, referred to so often in this history, they say had the best hand for salting pork of any woman in all of La Mancha.' "
>
> When I heard him say "Dulcinea of Toboso," I was astounded and filled with anticipation, for it occurred to me that those volumes contained the history of Don Quixote. With this thought in mind, I urged him to read the beginning, which he did, extemporizing a translation of the Arabic into Castilian and saying that it said: *History of Don Quixote of La Mancha. Written by Cide Hamete Benegeli, an Arab Historian.*[6] (original italics)

This manuscript of *Don Quixote* within *Don Quixote* not only problematizes the attributability of the text, but also symbolizes the effacement of Cervantes himself, as both the narrator and the reader of *Don Quixote* now inhabit the memory of this Arab historian. It is then small wonder that Wordsworth turns the Spanish Quixote into an Arabian knight.

Another reason for the Arabian identity of this knight may be because of Wordsworth's interest in *The Arabian Nights*, as he mentions that:

> I had a precious treasure at that time,
> A little yellow canvass-covered book,
> A slender abstract of the *Arabian Tales*;
> And when I learned, as now I first did learn
> From my companions in this new abode,
> That this dear prize of mine was but a block
> Hewn from a mighty quarry – in a word,
> That there were four large volumes, laden all
> With kindred matter – 'twas in truth to me

---

[6] Miguel de Cervantes Saavedra, *Don Quixote*, trans. Edith Grossman (New York: HarperCollins, 2003), Part 1, Chapter 9, p. 67. All the subsequent references to *Don Quixote* are based on this translation unless stated otherwise. In this translation, the narrator is described as obsessed with 'torn papers in the streets', while in John Rutherford's translation, he reads 'even scraps of paper lying in the gutter' (p. 74), both stressing the fragmented and non-attributable nature of the manuscript, which will be delved into in the following chapter.

A promise scarcely earthly. Instantly
I made a league, a covenant with a friend
Of my own age, that we should lay aside
The monies we possessed, and hoard up more,
Till our joint savings had amassed enough
To make this book our own.
(1805, Book 5, II. 460–73)

It is least surprising that he turns first Don Quixote, and then implicitly himself, into an Arab. Another indirect reference to *The Arabian Nights* is the setting of a rocky cave. This rocky cave immediately conjures up the image of Plato's allegorical cave mentioned in Book Seven of *The Republic*, which symbolizes, among many things, a search for truth outside the cave. At the same time, this rocky cave also alludes to the stories in *The Arabian Nights*, like 'The Second Kalandar's Tale', 'Sindbad's Second Voyage', 'Alaeddin or the Wonderful Lamp', and 'Ali Baba and the Forty Thieves', all of which involve adventures and treasures stored in a cave. Especially in the story 'Ali Baba and the Forty Thieves', the cave and the treasures are unlocked by the magic formula 'open sesame'. In Wordsworth's reading of Don Quixote, Don Quixote is the magic formula 'open sesame' and it is through him that the secrets in the dream and in the cave are unlocked.

But what is this Arabian knight doing in Wordsworth's reading of Don Quixote? Besides his lance, he is holding a stone and a shell, which represent geometry and poetry respectively ('On poetry and geometric truth', line 65).[7] In Hillis Miller's view, a stone, when unhallowed, uncarved or uninscribed, refers only to itself and thus resists signification and displacement. It is like a blank face or a sheet of paper, commanding space by its fixity. It symbolizes permanence, composure and peace. However, the rocky cave in which the narrator (or the narrator's friend in 1805 edition) sits by the sea-side is in the form of a shell, symbolizing a figure for subjectivity looking out on the world. In this sense, a shell represents human consciousness, temporality, the power of sign making and of sign reading. At the same time, the shell in this dream of Arabian Quixote also stands for an apocalyptic call, an apocalyptic warning, an end-of-the-world reminder. An apocalyptic scene has actually been set before this dream:

Should the whole frame of earth by inward throes
Be wrenched, or fire come down from far to scorch
Her pleasant habitations, and dry up
Old Ocean, in his bed left singed and bare
(1850, Book 5, ll. 30–33)

This apocalyptic scene comes in the form of fire, drying up 'Old Ocean', which symbolizes the source of life. In this light, this apocalypse can be regarded as a

[7] J. Hillis Miller in his book *The Linguistic Moment: From Wordsworth to Stevens* (New Jersey: Princeton University Press, 1985), Chapter 2, pp. 78–113, gives a detailed and insightful analysis of this Arabian dream and the implications of the stone and the shell.

destruction of the origin, the coming of the end to efface the beginning. While this apocalypse comes in the form of fire, the next two scenes come in the form of deluge. When held to the ear, the shell, through sounds of an 'unknown tongue', articulates 'a loud prophetic blast of harmony' 'which foretold / Destruction to the children of the earth / By deluge' (ll. 93–8). Another apocalyptic image is unveiled[8] near the end of this dream also in the form of flooding: 'it is … the waters of the deep / Gathering upon us' (ll. 130–31), 'the fleet waters of a drowning world' (l. 137). The narrator is sitting by the sea-side in a rocky cave, watching the coming of the apocalypse in the form of flooding. This apocalyptic nature of the shell and hence of poetry is what the narrator wants to foreground. The shell is portrayed as 'of a surpassing brightness' (l. 80), as 'something of more worth' (l. 89), 'so beautiful in shape, in colour so resplendent' (ll. 90–91). While the stone holds 'acquaintance with the stars' and weds 'soul to soul in purest bond / Of reason, undisturbed by space or time' (ll. 103–5), the shell is a god, is many gods, having 'voices more than all the winds, with power / To exhilarate the spirit, and to soothe, / Through every clime, the heart of human kind' (ll. 106–9). It reveals the very essence of poetry, and hence writing: it is simultaneously harmonious, soothing and godly on the one hand, and prophetic, apocalyptic and deadly on the other.

The stone and the shell embody several levels of allegorization. In the first place, geometry and poetry are allegorized as the stone and the shell, respectively. Then the stone and the shell are further displaced as two books (l. 102). However, this displacement is problematized in that the narrator cannot decide whether they are the stone and the shell or whether they are books. It seems they are simultaneously the stone and the shell on the one hand and the books on the other: 'although I plainly saw / The one to be a stone, the other a shell; / Nor doubted once but that they both were books' (ll. 111–13). They now become undecidable. This undecidability is also found in the Arabian knight: 'He rode, I keeping pace with him; and now / He, to my fancy, had become the knight / Whose tale Cervantes tells; yet not the knight, / But was an Arab of the desert too; / Of these was neither, and was both at once' (ll. 121–5). This mysterious person is both the knight and not the knight Don Quixote, both an Arab and not an Arab. This undecidability upsets the displacement and hence makes it non-displaceable, and at the same time, this undecidability may be regarded as another displacement of the original displacement, producing a displacement of displacement, like another trace on a palimpsestic parchment.

But what does the Arabian knight do to the stone and the shell / the two books. In line 102 (1850 edition), he is described as going to bury these two books. The act of burying the books can be read as a fear of losing them, an attempt to avoid the effacement of writing and to preserve the manuscripts. This foregrounds the importance of writing and manuscripts, and the importance of the archive for

[8] Derrida in his essay 'Of an Apocalyptic Tone Recently Adopted in Philosophy' (in *Derrida and Negative Theology*, ed. by Harold Coward & Toby Foshay (Albany: State University of New York, 1992, Chapter 2, pp. 25–72) points out that the Greek word *apokalupsis* means disclosure, discovery, uncovering, unveiling, the veil lifted from about the thing: first of all, man's or woman's sex, but also their eyes or ears.

preserving manuscripts. More importantly, this reveals one function of the archive – the preservation of manuscripts in fear of their effacement.

1.2. González Echevarría: Origin, Secrecy and Power

With the purpose for preservation, the archive is a place for hoarding of manuscripts, whether they are complete or incomplete, finished or unfinished. It is also a place accessible to only a privileged few and it is closely intertwined with the issues of origin, secrecy and power. The word 'archive' comes from the Greek word 'archeion' which means the residence or the house of the magistrates and so, it is associated with the 'archons', the ruler. The word 'archive' is also derived from the word 'arkhē', which means both commencement and commandment:

> *Arkhē*, we recall, names at once the *commencement* and the *commandment*. This name apparently coordinates two principles in one: the principle according to nature or history, *there* where things *commence* – physical, historical, or ontological principle – but also the principle according to the law, *there* where men and gods *command*, *there* where authority, social order are exercised, *in this place* from which *order* is given – nomological principle. (Derrida 1996, 1) (original italics)

The archive thus is a place from which things commence, a place of origin, and at the same time, it is a place in which commands and orders are decreed, a place of law and authority. In this regard, the archive is a place for the interplay of the ontological principle and the nomological principle, the force of origin and the force of law. These two principles or forces are intertwined into one – an archival principle from which the significance of manuscripts the archive houses is inseparable. The archon's commanding power relies on the official manuscripts filed in his house and on his position of a guardian of these manuscripts. Because of this, the guardian of the archive has the power to interpret the archive and the manuscripts and thus the power to speak the law: to recall and impose the law, to originate and enforce the law, to commence and command by law.

The archive is patriarchal in nature because of its power to speak the law, to speak for the law and to speak of the law. It is both a commanding power and a power of interpretation. The very concept of the archive embeds the notion of masculinity in it. It is a place for safeguarding its secrecy, origin and authority by a patriarchal archon. In this sense, the patriarchal archive, or the 'patriarchive' as Derrida calls it (1996, 4), is a process of homogenization and centralization, hence resisting the heterogeneous other. The act of archiving manuscripts inevitably involves categorization, which is a process of exclusion, demarcating what should and should not be housed in the archive.

This attempt of homogenization and centralization through the archive can be found in the Spanish history. The word 'archive' entered Spanish in 1490,[9] during

[9] González Echevarría's *Myth and archive*, p. 31, reads: 'Corominas writes: "*Archivo*, 1490, Tomado del latín tardío *archivum*, y éste del griego *archeion* 'residencia

the reign of the Catholic Kings. The year 1479 is important as it marks the union of the two kingdoms, Castile and Aragon. Isabella I was the queen of Castile from 1474 to 1504, and of Aragon from 1479 to 1504 after marrying Ferdinand II of Aragon in October 1469. This marks a permanent union of Spain and the beginning of an overseas empire in the New World.[10] In 1492, Christopher Columbus was granted the support from Isabella I and Ferdinand II and set out to discover a new route for his expedition to 'discover' America. Since then, the modern period of Spanish imperial expansion commenced. González Echevarría points out the important role the concept of the archive plays in the founding of the modern state (González Echevarría 1998, 32). The Simancas Archive near Valladolid in Spain is a voluminous archive in Europe, and was an archival project masterminded by Charles V and finished by Philip II. These kings were most interested in paper and manuscripts, especially maps. Because of this, Ferdinand II, Charles I and Philip II are called 'paper-monger kings' (González Echevarría 1998, 30). This Simancas Archive may represent not only these monarchs' desire for gathering information and preserving it in the form of manuscripts, but also their belief and attempt of building an empire held together by manuscripts and archives.

Among these 'paper-monger kings', Philip II is the most intriguing figure representing a strong desire for papers and for accumulation, preservation and manipulation of secrets and information. He preferred to rule his empire from behind a desk, leaving the legwork to his bureaucrats. The result was a government by paper.[11] From Madrid he ruled his empire through his personal control of official appointments and all forms of patronage. His subjects outside Castile never saw him. All work was done on paper, on the basis of 'consultas' – that is, memoranda, reports and advice presented to him by his ministers. He worked alone in his small office as his 'archive' in the gloomy magnificence of his monastic palace of El Escorial, which he built on the slopes of the Sierra de Guadarrama. From this archive, he made his decisions as much as he deferred them. He always painstakingly pined for more information, hiding his inability to distinguish between the important and the trivial and above all, a temperamental unwillingness to make decisions. At the same time, he felt a sense of security among his State papers, although he burdened himself with reading, annotating

---

de los magistrados,' 'archivo,' derivado de *arkhe* 'mando,' 'magistratura'." ("Taken from late Latin *archivum*, and this from the Greek *archeion*, 'residence of the magistrates,' 'archive,' derived from *arkhe* 'command,' 'magistracy.' (original italics) and on p. 191, Joan Corominas, *Breve diccionario etimológico de la lenngua castellana.* (Madrid: Gredos, 1961).

[10] From "Isabella I" *Encyclopædia Britannica* from Encyclopædia Britannica Online. http://search.eb.com/eb/article?eu=43808.

[11] J.H. Elliott, *Spain and its World, 1500–1700* (New Haven and London: Yale University Press, 1989), p. 15. See also J.H. Elliott, *Imperial Spain, 1469–1716* (London: Edward Arnold (Publishers) Ltd., 1963), pp. 251–2.

and amending them continually. Because of this, the workings of the government were inevitably slowed down.[12]

The Simancas Archive project by Charles V and Philip II was originally a castle for prisoners and was turned into an archive in 1539 (and it is by no means a coincidence that Cervantes started writing *Don Quixote* in prison) (González Echevarría 1998, 18). Because of this archival project, Spain possessed a central archive for a bureaucratic state and the archive functioned as a central repository for manuscripts and documents kept and issued for the running of the government and the ruling of the country. The paper-monger kings' archival policies mirror Spain's patriarchal desire for domination and homogenization. In 1492, Spain issued an order that all Jews and Arabs had either to convert to Christianity or to leave Spain. If it is viewed in terms of patriarchal attempt to sustain its racial purity, what Spain was doing was to exclude the racial and religious other. Ironically, this is also a period in which Spain sent out Christopher Columbus and hence, triggered off its project of colonizing the others. The archive in this light is closely related to colonization. If all these are regarded as a patriarchal drive for ideological homogenization and cultural hegemony, the archival policies are also part of this undertaking.

The concept of the archive is not only related to cultural retention, but also concerned about the origin. It is a place housing the original manuscripts and documents and thus it is a source of power, authority and interpretation. This source of origin is also associated with writing. González Echevarría remarks that the archive is connected with the origin of the novel, as the setting up of the Simancas Archive in 1539 coincided with the appearance of the first Spanish novel *Lazarillo de Tormes*, published in 1554 (González Echevarría 1998, 29–30). The novel *Lazarillo de Tormes*, like its picaro hero, pretends to be something else. It is narrated as if it was written for a judge. The story starts with Lazarillo's account of his father's death in war after being banished by the law, his mother's inability to support him and his subsequent placement in the care of a blind beggar. Lazarillo, the hero of this picaresque novel, is a criminal and rascal and the whole novel is about his life and how he escapes punishment. This is a stark contrast to the novel of chivalry in which the hero is usually a knight or a gallant gentleman performing brave deeds. Both the archive and the novel appeared at the same period of time and were part of the same discourse of the modern state. This not only reveals the importance of the concept of the archive for Latin American literature, but also affirms González Echevarría view that Latin America, as a historical entity, was not merely 'discovered' by Columbus, but, like the novel, was created in the archive (González Echevarría 1998, 32).

Besides being a place of origin and as a place for official and legal manuscripts, the archive is also the embodiment of law and power. This is especially related to the idea of remote empires which can only be mapped and documented in the

---

[12] J.H. Elliott, *Imperial Spain, 1469–1716*, p. 243. Also "Philip II" *Encyclopædia Britannica* from Encyclopædia Britannica Online. http://search.eb.com/eb/article?eu=61178.

archive at a distance from the territory. The archive, in this light, helps achieve remote control and administration.

The essence of this archive can be captured as follows:

> The Archive keeps, culls, retains, accumulates, and classifies, like its institutional counterpart. It mounts up, amounts to the law, the law of fiction. Fictions are contained in an enclosure, a prisonhouse of narrative that is at the same time the origin of the novel. (González Echevarría 1998, 18)

It implies that the archive is not merely a place of secrecy, origin and power, but also a process of the institutional homogenization in terms of keeping, culling, retaining, accumulating and classifying. Furthermore, it is also closely related to the law of fiction and the origin of the novel, especially in the form of a 'prisonhouse of narrative'.

1.3. Foucault: Totalization and Paralysis

While González Echevarría stresses the archive as a place of secrecy, origin and power, Foucault, from sociological and epistemological perspectives, unveils the totalizing power and the homogenizing discourse of the archive by pointing out that the archive is a place for 'accumulation of time':

> … the idea of accumulating everything, of establishing a sort of general archive, the will to enclose in one place all times, all epochs, all forms, all tastes, the idea of constituting a place of all times that is itself outside of time and inaccessible to its ravages, the project of organizing in this way a sort of perpetual and indefinite accumulation of time in an immobile place, this whole idea belongs to our modernity. (Foucault 1986, 26)

The hegemonic nature of the archive is further revealed through its totalizing enclosure of everything, including 'all times, all epochs, all forms, all tastes'. This is a place centralizing and organizing everything it accumulates, including time, but at the same time, it is outside of time and immune to time's ravages.

In *The Archaeology of Knowledge*, Foucault stresses this theme of archival totalization, especially on the discursive level:

> Between the *language* (*langue*) that defines the system of constructing possible sentences, and the *corpus* that passively collects the words that are spoken, the *archive* defines a particular level: that of a practice that causes a multiplicity of statements to emerge as so many regular events, as so many things to be dealt with and manipulated. It does not have the weight of tradition; and it does not constitute the library of all libraries, outside time and place; nor is it the welcoming oblivion that opens up to all new speech the operational field of its freedom; between tradition and oblivion, it reveals the rules of a practice that enables statements both to survive and to undergo regular modification. It is *the*

> *general system of the formation and transformation of statements.* (Foucault 1972, 130) (original italics)

In Foucault's view, the archive stands outside any particular language system, beyond a language system of active construction of possible statements or to the passive collection of corpus. It is a place which allows the accumulation and emergence of multiplicity of statements to be dealt with and manipulated. It is not under the weight of tradition or not entirely oblivious or obliterating by nature, but it exists between tradition and oblivion by which statements are allowed to survive and to undergo modification. It belongs to tradition but not under the weight of it because the tradition that it belongs to is the remote past, not the present one. In Lyotard's terms, the archive is a space of disappropriated consciousness since the presenting present is also disappropriated as a presented present. It is not entirely oblivious in the sense that the fragmentary nature of the archive lies in its part-oblivion, which is also the power of its glamour, obscurity and phantasmal lure of the incomplete. By being situated between tradition and oblivion, the archive generates a system of not only formation, but also transformation of statements. This is the totalizing power of the archive through which domination is manifested. Because of this system generated by the archive, Foucault says that:

> [t]he archive is first the law of what can be said, the system that governs the appearance of statements as unique events. But the archive is also that which determines that all these things said do not accumulate endlessly in an amorphous mass, nor are they inscribed in an unbroken linearity, nor do they disappear at the mercy of chance external accidents; but they are grouped together in distinct figures, composed together in accordance with multiple relations, maintained or blurred in accordance with specific regularities; that which determines that they do not withdraw at the same pace in time, but shine, as it were, like stars, some that seem close to us shining brightly from afar off, while others that are in fact close to us are already growing pale. (Foucault 1972, 129)

The archive is the law of what can be said, represented and recorded, and because of this, it governs and guarantees the uniqueness of events. But Foucault points out that the archive can go beyond and does not follow an unbroken linearity, and that it will not disappear 'at the mercy of chance external accidents'. Instead, manuscripts, statements and meanings within the archive are categorized in accordance with multiple relations and can be maintained and preserved, or blurred and marginalized. Existing through the interplay among multiple relations, what is housed in the archive will not withdraw or disappear at the same pace in time. Instead, they are like stars, shining differently according to regularities and categorizations of the archive. Some shine brightly but actually are far away, while some close to us grow pale. The archive is like a cosmos in which each and every manuscript and meaning shines differently within the complex multiple relations not only among themselves, but also according to how they are categorized, used and interpreted.

In terms of the functions of the archive and the manuscripts housed in it, Foucault further comments that,

> The archive is not that which, despite its immediate escape, safeguards the event of the statement, and preserves, for future memories, its status as an escapee; it is that which, at the very root of the statement-event, and in that which embodies it, defines at the outset *the system of its enunciability*. Nor is the archive that which collects the dust of statements that have become inert once more, and which may make possible the miracle of their resurrection; it is that which defines the mode of occurrence of the statement-thing; it is *the system of its functioning*. Far from being that which unifies everything that has been said in the great confused murmur of a discourse, far from being only that which ensures that we exist in the midst of preserved discourse, it is that which differentiates discourses in their multiple existence and specifies them in their own duration. (Foucault 1972, 129) (original italics)

The archive embraces the uniqueness of events, but cannot safeguard or guarantee the event of the statement or preserve its status for future memories. The archive from the very beginning defines the system of its enunciability in which manuscripts and statements exist, like a cosmos which limits how far a star can shine. The archive creates its own cosmos in which its manuscripts' uniqueness is secured but their meanings, signification and status are dependent upon the system of their enunciability, that is, their position in the dominant discourse. The archive is more than merely to accumulate and collect the dust of statements or to provide a site for their resurrection, but is a system of functioning through which the mode of the statements' occurrence, their meanings and functions are defined. This is the defining power of the archive, its power to totalize, classify and define meanings. It differentiates different discourses and allows them to carry on to survive in their multiple existences and in their own duration.

Another aspect of the totalizing nature of the archive, Foucault points out, is its ability to create 'otherness':

> The analysis of the archive … involves a privileged region: at once close to us, and different from our present existence, it is the border of time that surrounds our presence, which overhangs it, and which indicates it in its otherness; it is that which, outside ourselves, delimits us. The description of the archive deploys its possibilities (and the mastery of its possibilities) on the basis of the very discourses that have just ceased to be ours; its threshold of existence is established by the discontinuity that separates us from what we can no longer say, and from that which falls outside our discursive practice; it begins with the outside of our own language; its locus is the gap between our own discursive practices. … it deprives us of our continuities; it dissipates the temporal identity in which we are pleased to look at ourselves when we wish to exorcise the discontinuities of history; … In this sense, the diagnosis does not establish the fact of our identity by the play of distinctions. It establishes that we are difference, that our reason is the difference of discourses, our history the difference of times, our selves the difference of masks. That difference, far from being the forgotten and recovered origin, is this dispersion that we are and make. (Foucault 1972, 130–31)

The archive is a homogenizing site creating not only the same, but also the other, a delimiting place classifying what should be inside and outside of it, and a demarcating threshold depriving us of continuity in terms of discursive practices. This sense of discontinuity of the archive is the upshot of its being a place for origin, secrecy and power. This homogenizing nature of the archive creates the commensurability, from which things and people are viewed as either commensurable or not. Bataille, who is in line with Foucault in this respect, says:

> *Homogeneity* signifies here the commensurability of elements and the awareness of this commensurability: human relations are sustained by a reduction to fixed rules based on the consciousness of the possible identity of delineable persons and situations; in principle, all violence is excluded from this course of existence. (Bataille 1985, 137–8) (original italics)

This commensurability is an underlying desire for conformity in ideology and a reconciliation of heterogeneous elements. The commensurability of the archive is also an active force homogenizing and totalizing what it houses instead of static accumulation and coexistence of hybrid entities.

This homogenizing cosmos of the archive can best be revealed by Melquíades' room for his manuscripts in García Márquez's *One Hundred Years of Solitude*. This novel is basically made up of two main stories – one has to do with the family and culminates in the birth of the child with the pig's tail, while the other is about the interpretation of Melquíades' manuscripts which Aureliano Segundo, José Arcadio Segundo and Aureliano try to decipher. One important aspect of Melquíades' room, according to González Echevarría (1998, 21), is the two different kinds of temporality inside and outside his archive. The time outside Melquíades' archive is circular:

> 'I know all of this by heart,' Úrsula would shout. 'It's as if time had turned around and we were back at the beginning.' (210)
>
> José Arcadio Segundo was still reading over the parchments. … When he recognized his great-grandmother's voice he turned his head toward the door, tried to smile, and without knowing it repeated an old phrase of Úrsula's.
>
> 'What did you expect?' he murmured. 'Time passes.'
>
> 'That's how it goes,' Úrsula said, 'but not so much.'
>
> When she said it she realized that she was giving the same reply that Colonel Aureliano Buendía had given in his death cell, and once again she shuddered with the evidence that time was not passing, as she had just admitted, but that it was turning in a circle. (361)

This circular temporality is an example of magical realism, revealing the mystery behind ordinary life, disrupting the linear progression of time and entailing the possibility of endless repetition without progress. At the same time, there is a temporal discontinuity between Melquíades' archive and the world outside. The time inside Melquíades' room never changes. It is always March, always Monday:

> No one had gone into the room again since they had taken Melquíades' body out and had put on the door a padlock whose parts had become fused together with rust. But when Aureliano Segundo opened the windows a familiar light entered that seemed accustomed to lighting the room every day and there was not the slightest trace of dust of cobwebs, with everything swept and clean, better swept and cleaner than on the day of the burial, and the ink had not dried up in the inkwell nor had oxidation diminished the shine of the metals nor had the embers gone out under the water pipe where José Arcadio Buendía had vaporized mercury. On the shelves were the books bound in a cardboard-like material, pale, like tanned human skin, and the manuscripts were intact. In spite of the room's having been shut up for many years, the air seemed fresher than in the rest of the house. Everything was so recent that several weeks later, when Úrsula went into the room with a pail of water and a brush to wash the floor, there was nothing for her to do. (199)

> In the small isolated room where the arid air never penetrated, nor the dust, nor the heat, both had the atavistic vision of an old man, his back to the window, wearing a hat with a brim like the wings of a crow who spoke about the world many years before they had been born. Both [that is, José Arcadio Segundo and Aureliano] described at the same time how it was always March there and always Monday… (375)

Melquíades' archive has its own time, which creates discontinuity with the temporal progression outside it. In this archive, Melquíades' mythical manuscripts and books shine like stars and will not 'disappear at the mercy of chance external accidents'. Because of the totalizing and homogenizing power of the archive, time accumulated becomes an eternal March and an eternal Monday.

1.4. Derrida: Burning Evil and Violence

While Foucault foregrounds the totalizing power of the archive by which things are kept intact, rigid and frozen, Derrida underlines archival violence and destructive force in *Archive Fever*. Its French title *Mal d'Archive* can be understood in two ways, as Rapaport points out. 'Mal d'archive' means there is certain evil in the archive, especially the one which is kept secret and preserved in the archive. However, 'mal d'archive' also refers to 'the feverish hunt for something in an archive that has presumably been lost or that has been kept secret' (Rapaport 2003, 77) and this *mal* is traumatic in nature:

> … it is a *mal* that relates directly to Derrida's spectral archive of the 1970s. Yet, it is a holocaust we could and probably should associate with the burning down of archives, and not just of Jewish books in Nazi demonstrations of the 1930s, but of archives like the Library of Alexandria, that, for Western civilization, is perhaps paradigmatic of archive trauma. … what is worse than the destruction

> of the archive by those who want to liquidate culture is their desire to archive their evil, to painstakingly record the physical destruction of the very people they execrate in order that future generations may inherit the legacy of their evil *as* evil. (Rapaport 2003, 77) (original italics)

This *mal d'archive* comes in the form of destruction, holocaust and feverish burning. This destructive force, violence of the archive, archival violence, targets not only the other in the form of an annihilating holocaust and cultural liquidation, but also itself, as Derrida says:

> … this three-named drive [i.e. sometimes death drive, sometimes aggression drive, sometimes destruction drive] is mute (*stumm*). It is at work, but since it always operates in silence, it never leaves any archives of its own. It destroys in advance its own archive, as if that were in truth the very motivation of its most proper movement. It works *to destroy the archive: on the condition of effacing* but also *with a view to effacing* its own "proper" traces – which consequently cannot properly be called "proper." It devours it even before producing it on the outside. This drive, from then on, seems not only to be anarchic, anarchontic (we must not forget that the death drive, originary though it may be, is not a principle, as are the pleasure and reality principles): the death drive is above all *anarchivic*, one could say, or *archiviolithic*. It will always have been archive-destroying, by silent vocation. (Derrida 1996, 10) (original italics and brackets)

> … right on that which permits and conditions archivization, we will never find anything other than that which exposes to destruction, and in truth menaces with destruction, introducing, *a priori*, forgetfulness and the archiviolithic into the heart of the monument. … The archive always works, and *a priori*, against itself. (Derrida 1996, 12) (original italics)

In the archive, there is already a drive which works against the memory of the archive and the very structure of the archive it comes from. This drive is simultaneously death, aggression and destruction. It is 'anarchivic', that is, 'anti-archive', because it works against itself, against the archive that it itself establishes, resulting in self-effacement and annihilation. The archive is also a place of violence that violates the stone on which law and writing are inscribed, and hence it is 'archiviolithic', etymologically meaning an archive that violates the stone (for law and writing). The archive is the residence of the archon and hence it requires an archon. This reveals the primacy of space in the archive in that, on the one hand, an archon is needed because of the existence of the archive, and on the other hand, the archive exemplifies the production of power based on the production of space, as implicated in Foucault's 'Of Other Spaces' (1986). But paradoxically, its archiviolithic nature effaces its own archon and so it lacks order or control (anarchic) and then anti-archon (anarchontic). It is without a ruler, a guardian of law or a law-maker or law-enforcer, and hence it is 'anarchic', which stresses the effacement of the archive itself. It is without and beyond rules and law, and hence it is 'anarchontic', which foregrounds the absence of the archon. At the same time, this 'anarchontic' drive also entails the absence of the rule, law or principle of being (*an*, without; *archōn*, to rule; *ōn* or *ont*, being). It is anti-ontology, against the law and principle of being. As such, Derrida claims that 'the death drive, originary though it may be, is not a principle, as are the pleasure and reality principles'. (Derrida 1996, 10)

What is a 'principle'? *OED* associates it with 1. a fascist patriarch; 2. law; 3. an origin, an originating source; 4. the concept of 'proper'; 5. theory (as 'in principle' means 'in theory'). The word 'principle', like the word 'principal', is derived from the root *princes*, which means 'first' or 'chief'. It is originating and self-originating, both within and outside the system that it constructs. But the archiviolithic drive of the archive is at the same time anarchontic, which means that the archive not only destroys itself, not only does it in advance, effacing its own 'proper' traces, but also violates the primary being, the originary law, the originating principle. In this regard, the death / aggression / destructive drive, this anarchontic drive in and of the archive, and hence the archive itself, are against the principle of the principles, against the primal principle, and against the principal principle.

The archive destroys itself, which is predestined at the beginning of the creation of the archive. The archive, together with the manuscripts housed in it, exposes itself to destruction, forgetfulness and effacement. This archiviolithic force 'leaves no monument, it bequeaths no document of its own' and it 'leaves nothing of its own behind' (Derrida 1996, 11), not even its own 'proper' traces. This evil of the archive, through its archiviolithic and also anarchontic forces, feverishly burns its own archive into cinders, leaving non-traceable traces. The distinction between death and the archive does not seem to hold. Death manifests itself as the anarchivic, archiviolithic, anarchic and anarchontic forces within an archive and it is its own archive, burning itself to violate and go beyond the principle of the principles so as to erase any possibility of being a principle. Both are destruction without return,[13] as Derrida puts it:

> But from the moment this concept of cinders becomes the figure for everything that precisely loses its figure in incineration and thus in a certain disappearance of the support or of the body whose memory is kept by the cinders, at that moment cinders is no longer a determined concept. It is a trope that comes to take the place of everything that disappears without leaving an identifiable trace. The difference between the trace 'cinder' and other traces is that the body of which cinders is the trace has totally disappeared, it has totally lost its contours, its form, its colors, its natural determination. Non-identifiable. And forgetting itself is forgotten. Everything is annihilated in the cinders. Cinders is the figure of that of which not even cinders remains in a certain way. There is nothing that remains of it. (Derrida 1995, 391)

This destruction of the archive's own self does not leave anything behind, not even an identifiable, traceable trace. If the archive is meant for preservation, what is preserved is only the memory of cinders. If the archive is ideologically

---

[13] The idea is from Derrida's *Cinders* trans. Ned Lukacher (Lincoln: University of Nebraska Press, 1991).

patriarchal in nature, what is also inherent in itself at the very beginning is the end, the death and the untraceable cinders of patriarchy. In other words, the genesis of the archive already contains its apocalypse. It is because of the foreshadowing of this apocalypse within the archive that the Arabian Quixote in Wordsworth's texts buries both the stone and the shell underground in the hope of preserving writing against the onslaught of the apocalyptic flood.

Besides manifesting itself in the form of apocalyptic and traumatic destruction, *mal d'archive* also comes in the form of spectrality, which is, according to Derrida, the very structure of the archive:

> … the structure of the archive is *spectral*. It is spectral *a priori*: neither present nor absent "in the flesh," neither visible nor invisible, a trace always referring to another whose eyes can never be met, no more than those of Hamlet's father, thanks to the possibility of a visor. Also, the spectral motif stages this disseminating fission from which the archontic principle, and the concept of the archive, and the concept in general suffer, from the principle on. (Derrida 1996, 84–5) (original italics)

The spectral archive defies presence and absence, visibility and invisibility. Derrida points out that the trace of the spectrality of the archive refers to 'another whose eyes can never be met'. This spectral archive effects a 'disseminating fission', the splitting of and during dissemination within itself. It is worth reiterating that this is the collapse of the archontic principle which is the principle of the ruler, and hence the archive is anarchontic and anarchic. The concept of the archive also collapses due to its self-destructive, self-effacing nature and hence the archive is archiviolithic. Ultimately, the concept in general no longer holds and the disseminating fission, that is, the splitting of the concept during its dissemination, evaporates the concept into thin air, not allowing any signification to take place.

The complexity of the archive in terms of evil and violence is constituted by its holocaustic annihilation of the other and cultural liquidation and by its archiviolithic and anarchontic destruction. This spectral archive is traumatic in nature as its evil lies in the annihilation of not only itself and the otherness within itself, but the other and the otherness outside itself as well. In other words, archivization is synonymous with traumatization and annihilation. The *mal d'archive* lies not only in its death drive for silencing and effacing the heterogeneous, but also in its paralyzing force petrifying both memory and life. Hence, the horror of the archive is the possibility of the archivization of the evil attempts to liquidate culture and to physically annihilate the other and as a result, what the future generations inherit from this archive is evil. It may be that because the archive is archiviolithic from the very beginning, this traumatic possibility, this possibility of trauma can be avoided. Nobody can tell if this evil of the archive can be burned into cinders so that no trace will be left behind and that not only this self-annihilation, but also the evil of the traumatic archive, will never be repeated.

As Wordsworth's cave implies, the archive is inherent with a process of preservation and a force of apocalyptic destruction. As González Echevarría points out, the archive is a place of patriarchal and centralizing domination in terms of secrecy, law and origin. As Foucault asserts, it is totalizing through a textual systemization of its own enunciability. As Derrida reveals, it is destructive and ghostly, and as Rapaport suggests, it is traumatic. The importance of the concept of the archive runs parallel with its complexity.

Another way of looking at the complexity of the archive is that it can refer to an establishment or institution, like a place for collection of manuscripts, and thus, metaphorically, a library or a police record room can also be regarded as an archive. But the concept of the archive can also refer to the practice of control and categorization, and hence it can be considered an agent of ideology, symbolizing authority, secrecy and the power of the origin. To a certain extent, it may be difficult to grasp this apparently simple, yet highly complex concept, but it is without doubt that the archive is homogenizing, paralyzing, archiviolithic, spectral and traumatic. However, the intrigue of the archive is that such a centralizing and paralyzing structure of the archive houses manuscripts, which defy such a kind of structure, and this is the focus of Chapter 2.

Chapters 3 and 4 look at the concepts of the archive and the manuscript in Cervantes, with reference to *Don Quixote* and *Exemplary Stories*. In these manuscripts of Cervantes, Don Quixote attempts to construct a reality out of a past which has gone and which is out-of-date. In other words, his anachronistic utopian knight-errantry can be regarded as a kind of writing within his archive of memory. At the same time, the importance of a seductive female narrator as a destabilizing and liberating force and the concept of tropelía will be discussed in Cervantes' 'The Dialogue of the Dogs' and 'The Glass Graduate' and Don Quixote's adventure in the Cave of Montesinos. This theme of Cervantes is so important that the writings of Borges, Puig and García Márquez can be considered as its continuity, application and modification. In Part III, the shadow of Cervantes upon these three writers will be traced along this line. Chapter 5 is on Borges's raiding of the library, Chapter 6 on Puig's raiding of the archives of the discourse of homosexuality, the Hollywood 'B' movies and police records, and Chapter 7 on García Márquez's raiding of the archive as a story unable to give a plot. These three raiders and writers of the archive are in the shadow of Cervantes, with the spectre of Cervantes behind them when writing and raiding the lost archive of Don Quixote. The concluding Chapter 8 will look at the concept of the archive in the technological age, especially in terms of electronic archivization and globalization as a new form of hegemony.

Chapter 2
'Naturally, a Manuscript'

Time hath, my lord, a wallet at his back
Wherein he puts alms for oblivion,
A great-siz'd monster of ingratitudes.
Those scraps are good deeds past, which are devour'd
As fast as they are made, forgot as soon
As done. ...

Shakespeare[1]

Naturally, a Manuscript

Eco[2]

This living hand, now warm and capable
Of earnest grasping, would, if it were cold
And in the icy silence of the tomb,
So haunt thy days and chill thy dreaming nights
That thou would wish thine own heart dry of blood,
So in my veins red life might stream again,
And thou be conscience-calm'd. See, here it is –
I hold it towards you.

Keats[3]

The archive is a place of its own traumatic evil, self-destructive violence and paralyzing totalization. However, it is further complicated by what it is supposed to house – the manuscript, which is inseparable from it. It is because of the nature of the manuscript in the archive, which runs counter to that of the archive, that the archive becomes a highly paradoxical site. But what is a manuscript? At first glance, a manuscript is different from a book in that the former lacks a definite physical form while the latter is usually in a 'bound' form with covers. But this distinction becomes problematic once the book is in fragments, or once part of it is gone, resulting in its being non-attributable. In other words, it may be difficult to distinguish a manuscript from a book if the latter has the characteristics of the former.

---

[1] William Shakespeare, *Troilus and Cressida*, ed. Kenneth Palmer (The Arden Shakespeare) (London: Routledge, 1989), Act 3, Scene 3, ll. 145–50.

[2] Umberto Eco, *The Name of the Rose*, trans. William Weaver (London: Minerva, 1992), the epigraph.

[3] John Keats, 'This living hand, now warm and capable' in *John Keats: Complete Poems*, ed. Jack Stillinger (Cambridge, MA: The Belknap Press of Harvard University Press, 1982), p. 384.

2.1. Melquíades' Non-iterable Parchments

As mentioned in Chapter 1, García Márquez's *One Hundred Years of Solitude* concerns the deciphering of Melquíades' mythical manuscript. This is first attempted by Aureliano Segundo, then by José Arcadio Segundo and Aureliano and finally by Aureliano Babilonia. In this mythical manuscript, first of all, its authorship resists the effacement of the devouring time and second, this manuscript arrests time and stops all the clocks. Inside the archive where Melquíades' manuscripts are housed, the time is 'always March there and always Monday' (375). Time no longer moves, but is frozen and petrified. This challenges the notion of the progression of time and hence its temporal linearity. This arrest of time contrasts with the temporal circularity outside the manuscripts and Melquíades' archive (210 and 361). Third, this defiance of the temporal linearity can be regarded as an attempt to free man from the confinement of chronometric time. According to Octavio Paz,

> when man was exiled from that eternity in which all times were one, he entered chronometric time and became a prisoner of the clock and the calendar. As soon as time was divided up into yesterday, today and tomorrow, into hours, minutes and seconds, man ceased to be one with time, ceased to coincide with the flow of reality. (Paz 1985, 209)

In this regard, there is a kind of eternity in Melquíades' archive in which all times are one. When Melquíades' eternal manuscripts are deciphered by Aureliano Babilonia, when the ciphers of these manuscripts are emptied out by interpretation, it is also the end of the narrative and the end of narration, as described at the end of the novel:

> Before reaching the final line, however, he had already understood that he would never leave that room, for it was foreseen that the city of mirrors (or mirages) would be wiped out by the wind and exiled from the memory of men at the precise moment when Aureliano Babilonia would finish deciphering the parchments, and that everything written on them was unrepeatable since time immemorial and forever more, because races condemned to one hundred years of solitude did not have a second opportunity on earth. (447–8)

The name 'Babilonia', which comes from the word 'Babel', symbolizes a plurality of languages and a state of heterogeneous chaos. This reference to the Tower of Babel implies the fact that interpretation may manifest itself in different forms and directions, but the manuscript becomes 'unrepeatable' once it is interpreted in one particular way. The manuscript is dead and petrified when it is deciphered, because one single interpretation means the exclusion and elimination of other interpretations through the process of homogenization. Like races that are 'condemned to one hundred years of solitude'[4] and will not have 'a second opportunity on earth',

---

4 A more detailed discussion on 'solitude' can be found in Chapter 6.

the act of interpretation excludes and precludes the second opportunity of interpretation. This, at the same time, can be regarded as a critique of the post-colonial condition embodied in such a homogenizing and interpretive endeavour. Such a paralyzing and totalizing interpretation will only consolidate the linguistic representations of the exotic 'other', resulting in the effacement of hybridity and cultural polyvalency. In other words, this homogenizing interpretation does not allow plurality of meanings. This also reveals the process of homogenization or exclusion of the others once the meaning of the manuscript is stabilized.

One way of evading the end of narration and the paralysis of meaning is through the fragmentation of the manuscript. There is an intricate and close relationship between the manuscript and the wind. The last paragraph of the novel abounds with images of wind. When Aureliano is deciphering Melquíades' manuscripts, the wind is gradually gaining force:

> At that point, impatient to know his own origin, Aureliano skipped ahead. Then the wind began, warm, incipient, full of voices from the past, the murmurs of ancient geraniums, sighs of disenchantment that preceded the most tenacious nostalgia. He did not notice it … He was so absorbed that he did not feel the second surge of wind either as its cyclonic strength tore the doors and windows off their hinges, pulled off the roof of the east wing, and uprooted the foundations. … Macondo was already a fearful whirlwind of dust and rubble being spun about by the wrath of the biblical hurricane when Aureliano skipped eleven pages so as not to lose time with facts he knew only too well, and he began to decipher the instant that he was living, deciphering it as he lived it, prophesying himself in the act of deciphering the last page of the parchments, as if he were looking into a speaking mirror. (447)

Aureliano's deciphering the meanings and secrets of the manuscript coincides with the moment when the wind blows fiercely. It seems the wind is sending the messages and interpretations hidden in the manuscript away in the manner as Sibyl does when she is prophesying, which is described in Virgil's *The Aeneid*[5]

---

[5] Virgil (Publius Vergilius Maro), *The Aeneid*, trans. Jackson Knight (Harmondsworth: Penguin Books, 1958), Book 3, p. 88, which reads:

> 'Then, having reached Italy, you shall first visit the city of Cumae where lie ghostly lakes amid Avernus' whispering forests. There shall you see a frantic maiden-prophetess who from deep within a cavern of rock foretells the decrees of Destiny. She commits words to writing by making marks on leaves; afterwards she sorts into order all the prophecies which she has written on them, and allows their messages to remain, a closed secret, in her cave. There they stay, all in order and motionless; but if once the hinge-post turns and even a slight wind strikes them, the delicate leaves are disturbed by the door's movement, and the prophetess never afterwards thinks of catching them as they flit within the rock-hollow, or of putting them together again into prophecies.'

and Book 6, p. 149, which reads:

and in Dante's *Paradise* of *The Divine Comedy.*[6] The moment writing is marked on the leaves is the moment it is scattered by the wind, and it is also the moment of its dissemination, disappearance and oblivion. Everything written has gone already and writing is always an ephemeral act. The moment it is written is the moment it is lost. It also means that the manuscript is an inherently incomplete event. The manuscript is never totalizing or totalizable. In the case of Melquíades' manuscripts, this happens simultaneously at another level. The wind blows with the act of interpreting and deciphering the mythical manuscripts, making both the secret messages hidden in the manuscripts and the interpretations of them ephemeral. Hence, everything written on them is unrepeatable. This is the unrepeatability not only of the ephemeral writing on the manuscript, but also of its interpretation.

In this mythical manuscript, writing and interpretation are fleeting and unrepeatable. The act of interpretation means the end of the manuscript and writing is an act of disappearance. But what about a mad manuscript, a manuscript about madness?

2.2. A Madman's Manuscript

In Dickens' *The Posthumous Papers of the Pickwick Club*, Volume 1, Chapter 11, Mr. Pickwick gets hold of a madman's manuscript from an old clergyman. This manuscript gives an autobiographical account of a nameless person and the narrative is highly coherent in terms of both chronology and causality. In terms of the former, the madman starts narrating his autobiography with his awareness of his madness, then his marriage. Soon after marriage, he realizes his wife's and his in-laws' monetary motive behind this marriage, so he kills first his wife, and then one of his brothers-in-law. His madness inevitably leads to violence and murder. In terms of causality, the narrative of the manuscript states the reasons for his deeds. His madness is a hereditary one, and he has been continually hearing voices and seeing spirits which goad him to kill his wife ('At last the old spirits who had been with me so often before, whispered in my ear that the time was come, and thrust the open razor into my hand.') (152). In this regard, the narrative of this manuscript is far from a madman's. In this madman's manuscript, everything is spelled out and no deciphering work is required. However, there is a discrepancy between madness and violence on the one hand and the logical and coherent narrative of this manuscript on the other. In other words, the form is not in line with the content. This may be another kind of madness: a madman speaking a logical language, coping well with Lacanian 'symbolic order' and the patriarchal system in terms of chronology and causality. But is he really mad if he is capable

'Only, pray, do not commit your prophecies to leaves, for they might fly in disorder as playthings for the grasping winds …'

[6] Dante Alighieri, *The Divine Comedy Vol. III: Paradise*, trans. Mark Musa (Harmondsworth: Penguin Books, 1986), Canto 33, ll. 65–6.

of doing so? It is more like an implicit critique of the distinction between the sane and the insane in terms of narrative and narratorship.

What is the secret of this manuscript? The secret of the male anonymous narrator of this manuscript is his madness, which he is at pains to repress and deny. But ironically, the manuscript opens with an affirmative phrase 'Yes! – a madman's!' His madness is announced and foretold right at the beginning of the manuscript, which not only frames his behaviour but also manipulates and restricts the reader's interpretation of the manuscript. The more he denies his madness, the madder he becomes or appears to be. Likewise, no matter how coherent and logical the madman's narrative is, he is after all a madman, being 'peeped at like a wild lion through the iron bars' (150), always under surveillance of the others, always under a panoptical eye. This may mean that the attempt to construct a discourse of madness is in the first place a mad undertaking. This may also reveal that to incorporate a 'logical' and 'coherent' discourse of madness into an anonymous fragmented manuscript is another madness.

Running counter to the totalizing nature of the archive asserted by Foucault (discussed in Chapter 1), the nature of the manuscript is anonymous, unfinished and cryptic, which thus allows multiple interpretations. It is especially the case if the manuscript is about a heterogeneous subject like madness. This heterogeneity of the manuscript is doubled in *The Pickwick Papers* since this madman's manuscript is contained within another larger manuscript, that is, the manuscript of the Pickwick Club. However, does a madman have a voice of his own to narrate his history and life? Is he allowed to and is he able to do so? It is true that the phrase 'Yes! – a madman's!' does affirm his madness. But it may not be as simple as a self-affirmation. This phrase is at the same time a reply to an imaginary other, to an imaginary question. It is also doubtful if this reply is from the madman. The first paragraph starts with a madman and ends with the madhouse, suggesting that this manuscript is written in a madhouse:

> 'Yes! – a madman's! How that word would have struck to my heart, many years ago! How it would have roused the terror that used to come upon me sometimes; sending the blood hissing and tingling through my veins, 'till the cold dew of fear stood in large drops upon my skin, and my knees knocked together with fright! I like it now though. It's a fine name. Shew me the monarch whose angry frown was ever feared like the glare of a madman's eye – whose cord and axe, were ever half so sure as a madman's gripe. Ho! ho! It's a grand thing to be mad! to be peeped at like a wild lion through the iron bars – to gnash one's teeth and howl, through the long still night, to the merry ring of a heavy chain – and to roll and twine among the straw, transported with such brave music. Hurrah for the madhouse! Oh it's a rare place! (149–50)

It is ironic that the madman under the 'ring of a heavy chain', under other people's surveillance and being locked up exclaims 'hurrah for the madhouse' and says 'I like it now though. It's a fine name.' The madman is said to start liking the name given to him. But who does the naming? To what extent is this naming or this name proper? And under whose authority or in what authority is this naming done? If he is given a name, this shows that first the nameless person is given a new identity; second, if the madman's 'confession' is done under surveillance, there is a strong implication that his name is bestowed by the medical authority or by the police; and third, this name is a marker of difference, of being put under surveillance of the others, and of a heterogeneous position. In this sense, the act of naming is ideological and the name is nothing but a social construct.

It is also dubious that the madman will call his autobiographical account a madman's 'manuscript', not 'a madman's confession', or 'a madman's autobiography'. It seems that the first paragraph of the manuscript is written by somebody else as the last paragraph is written in a greatly different tone:

> … When I woke I found myself here – here in this gay cell where the sun-light seldom comes, and the moon steals in, in rays which only serve to show the dark shadows about me, and that silent figure in its old corner. When I lie awake, I can sometimes hear strange shrieks and cries from distant parts of this large place. What they are, I know not; but they neither come from that pale form, nor does it regard them. For from the first shades of dusk 'till the earliest light of morning, it still stands motionless in the same place, listening to the music of my iron chain, and watching my gambols on my straw bed. (156)

It is written in the present tense and the narrator is in a calm and watchful state of mood. The manuscript ends with a silence – the narrator is watching the 'pale form' that is standing motionless, listening and watching. In a word, he falls silent at the end of the manuscript. This is in contrast to the response which is assumed to be his. If so, the first paragraph may be written by the police or the medical authority of the madhouse. Even the clergyman who passes this manuscript to Mr. Pickwick is doubtful about its authenticity:

> 'Then here,' said the old gentleman, 'is a little manuscript, which I had hoped to have the pleasure of reading to you myself. I found it on the death of a friend of mine – a medical man, engaged in our County Lunatic Asylum – among a variety of papers, which I had the option of destroying or preserving, as I thought proper. I can hardly believe that the manuscript is genuine, though it certainly is not in my friend's hand. However, whether it be the genuine production of a maniac, or founded upon the ravings of some unhappy being, which I think more probable, read it, and judge for yourself.' (144–5)

This reveals several characteristics of a manuscript. A manuscript is very often found by chance among various papers and hence it is no wonder this madman's manuscript is found among the Pickwick Papers, which are posthumous in nature. A manuscript always invites reading and interpretation and at the same time, because its authenticity is in question and because it is very often cryptic, reading or interpreting a manuscript is difficult. It is no wonder that this madman's manuscript is handed to Mr. Pickwick by a clergyman, who is normally assumed to have the ability and knowledge to decipher and interpret manuscript. But now, even the old clergyman is in doubt about the authenticity of this manuscript.

The beginning phrase 'Yes! – a madman's!' is not only an affirmation of the madman's heterogeneous status and a reply, but also a repetition. It repeats the title 'A Madman's Manuscript' in an elliptical way. In repetition, the repeated has a weakening effect upon the first. Freud, in 'The Uncanny' (1919) elucidates this problematic relation between the original and the repetition in terms of the double:

> ... we have characters who are to be considered identical because they look alike. ... the subject identifies himself with someone else, so that he is in doubt as to which his self is, or substitutes the extraneous self for his own. In other words, there is a doubling, dividing and interchanging of the self. And finally there is the constant recurrence of the same thing – the repetition of the same features or character-traits or vicissitudes, of the same crimes, or even the same names through several consecutive generations. (Freud, Standard Edition Vol. XVII, 234)

In this sense, repetition or doubling simultaneously constructs and destabilizes identity. The doubling of the term 'madman' problematizes the relationship between the title and the first phrase of the manuscript, between the first and the second. It is never certain whether the madman's newly given identity is constructed by the title, or his madmanhood, his heterogeneous position of a madman constructs the title. As it is rarely the case that a madman will be given a voice, as the narrative style of the first paragraph is in stark contrast with the last one, and as even the old clergyman fails to affirm the authenticity of this madman's manuscript, it is highly likely that the beginning of the manuscript is false. In this sense, it is a manuscript without a genuine beginning. It is a non-originating manuscript.

This manuscript is of special narrative interest in that it offers no beginning, while it has not only one but four conclusions. There is a conclusion at the end of the manuscript in which the madman remains silent, only watching the 'pale form' standing motionless, listening and watching. Another conclusion can be found in the supplementary paragraph after the manuscript in another person's handwriting, which functions as a meta-narrative of the manuscript. After this extra, supplemental ending is Mr. Pickwick's conclusion of the manuscript, but his conclusion is made by a refusal to comment on this manuscript:

> Mr Pickwick's candle was just expiring in the socket, as he concluded the perusal of the old clergyman's manuscript … (156)

There is another conclusion which is placed right at the beginning of the manuscript. The first phrase 'Yes! – a madman's!' can be read as a conclusion of the whole manuscript.

Like Dickens' 'A Madman's Manuscript', James' *The Turn of the Screw* is also a non-originating manuscript with a problematic beginning. On one Christmas Eve, a group of friends gather around a fire in a country house outside London and entertain themselves by telling ghost stories, and a man named Douglas proposes to tell a true story about two children and a governess. He mentions that the manuscript

> is in old faded ink and in the most beautiful hand. ... A woman's. She has been dead these twenty years. She sent me the pages in question before she died. (146)

But this posthumous manuscript which is written by a female hand is kept and locked in a drawer at home in London. Inevitably, the listeners have to wait three days for the manuscript to arrive by post and ultimately, the manuscript is read in the fourth evening. This ghostly manuscript can originate only with and after deferment. Listeners have to be kept waiting for the manuscript to unfold and the journey into the manuscript begins with a delay. The narrator seems to imply the difficulty in beginning a manuscript by problematizing and postponing the origination of the manuscript.

2.3. A Manuscript of Impertinent Curiosity

This non-originating nature of the manuscript can also be found in *Don Quixote*. First, as discussed in the previous chapter, the narrator comes across a manuscript in Toledo by chance in which the story of Don Quixote is written. In this sense, the rest of Part 1 is one big manuscript found in Toledo. The translator opens the manuscript not on the first page, but in the middle, in medias res. The beginning is skipped and what is at issue is the middle. This loss of the beginning is further foregrounded when the discovery of this manuscript is narrated not at the beginning of the novel, but in the middle of *Don Quixote*. Second, the writing in the margin of this Toledo manuscript has a comical effect and is about Dulcinea, who has 'the best hand for salting pork' (67). Third, this writing in the margin comes in the form of annotation rather than ciphers. This supplementary writing in the margin captures the narrator's attention and causes him to purchase the manuscript as it is about Dulcinea, who is the motivating force for Don Quixote's adventures, knight-errantry, imagination and life. The narrator of *Don Quixote* desires to possess the manuscript (that he is narrating) and hopes to decipher the secrets of Don Quixote and Dulcinea. The manuscript, simultaneously non-originating and comical, arouses his desire for possession.

The title of this non-originating manuscript is identical to the novel's, but it is not sure if the former repeats the latter or vice versa. If the manuscript found has already stated the beginning of Don Quixote's history and adventures, the chapters of the novel before Part 1, Chapter 9 repeat the Toledo manuscript and maybe because of this, the translator and the narrator read the manuscript from the middle. It seems the origination of the manuscript problematizes the origination of the novel. This manuscript, like 'A Madman's Manuscript', offers a problematic beginning.

The influence of Cervantes' *Don Quixote* on Dickens' *The Pickwick Papers* is especially conspicuous when 'The Man Who Was Recklessly Curious' (Part 1, Chapters 33–5) in the former and 'A Madman's Manuscript' are juxtaposed. Both concern a manuscript found and both involve a clerical personnel – a priest reading aloud the manuscript to the others in *Don Quixote* and a clergyman bestowing the manuscript on Mr. Pickwick. In both cases, the priest and the clergyman are doubtful about the authenticity of the manuscript:

> "This novel seems fine," said the priest, "but I cannot persuade myself that it is true; if it is invented, the author invented badly, because no one can imagine any husband foolish enough to conduct the costly experiment that Anselmo did. If this occurred between a lover and his lady, it might be plausible, but between a husband and his wife it seems impossible; as for the manner in which it was told, I did not find it displeasing." (*Don Quixote*, 312–13)

> I [the clergyman] can hardly believe that the manuscript is genuine, though it certainly is not in my friend's hand. However, whether it be the genuine production of a maniac, or founded upon the ravings of some unhappy being, which I think more probable, read it, and judge for yourself. (*The Pickwick Papers*, 145)

Both result in death and both are manuscripts within a larger manuscript – a Toledo manuscript and the posthumous papers of the Pickwick Club.

While 'A Madman's Manuscript' is written allegedly by a madman, the manuscript of 'The Man Who Was Recklessly Curious' is about madness. The story goes as follows: when Don Quixote is put to bed, the innkeeper, in an attempt to prove that it is wrong of the priest to say books of chivalry should be burned because of their bad influences, invites him to read aloud a manuscript left behind by an anonymous traveller. This anonymous manuscript unfolds the close friendship between Anselmo and Lotario in Florence. Anselmo falls in love with a lady called Camila and asks Lotario to go and ask for her hand on his behalf. After marriage, he maintains a close relationship with Lotario and gradually, his desire to test Camila to see if she is really faithful to him gets the better of him. He pretends to be out of town, but sends Lotario to seduce Camila. The plan, however, goes awry and Lotario finds himself falling in love with Camila. As Anselmo does not come home to render help to deal with Lotario, Camila believes her husband does not really love her, so she gives in to Lotario. When Anselmo 'returns' home, Lotario and Camila try to keep Anselmo from finding out what is going on. Eventually, their guilty conscience torments them and they decide to leave Anselmo and the town, believing that Camila's maid, Leonela, is going to expose their affair to Anselmo. Camila flees to a convent, while Lotario joins the army. Anselmo dies of a broken heart, regretting his foolish curiosity that has caused so much trouble. Lotario is killed in battle soon after and Camila, like Anselmo, dies 'in the pitiless embrace of sorrow and melancholy' (312).

This manuscript depicts a madness of an uncontrollable desire of voyeurism. This madness described in the manuscript is unfolded when Don Quixote is asleep. He does wake up once and because of this, the story is interrupted. But the storytelling resumes its momentum when Don Quixote falls asleep again. What this reveals is that there are two kinds of madness, Don Quixote's and Anselmo's. Anselmo is mad right at the beginning when his curious desire to test Camila's fidelity gets the better of him. He is mad when he talks Lotario into asking for the hand of Camila on his behalf and later seducing Camila. He is also mad when he gives up the chance to come forth to tell Camila the whole truth.

Before Anselmo and Camila's matrimonial relationship comes the implied homosociality between Anselmo and Lotario. Though it is not stated explicitly, it is implied that Anselmo wants his very best friend Lotario to sleep with Camila. If Lotario is Anselmo's double, does it mean that when Lotario sleeps with Camila, it also represents that Anselmo sleeps with Camila? Lotario makes reference to Christianity to underline how husband and wife are united into one flesh after marriage:

> … when the divine sacrament of marriage was established, with bonds so strong that death alone can undo them. And this miraculous sacrament is so strong and powerful that it makes one flesh of two different people, and in virtuous spouses it does even more, for although they have two souls, they have only one will. And from this it follows that since the flesh of the wife is one with the flesh of the husband, any stain that besmirches her, or any defect that appears in her, redounds to the flesh of the husband even if he has not given her … any reason for her wickedness. (282)

In matrimony, husband and wife are one flesh. If Lotario sleeps with Camila, does it mean that Lotario sleeps with Anselmo through Camila as a substitute? Does this reveal Anselmo's unconscious desire to sleep with Lotario? But why does Anselmo want his friend to sleep with his wife? If husband and wife are one flesh and one body, the defilement of the wife's body also means the defilement of the husband's. By asking his double, Lotario to defile his wife Camila, Anselmo is defiling his own body, as Lotario is his double and Camila is his own flesh and body.

Anselmo's madness is destructive as it defiles and destroys not only Anselmo himself, but also the others. In this regard, Anselmo's madness is more dangerous than Don Quixote's madness, which is a chivalrous attempt to free other people. Anselmo's case can be read in the light of Spain's attempt in 1492 to order all Jews and Arabs either to convert to Christianity or to leave Spain as a way to sustain its racial and religious purity by excluding the others. If so, first of all, Spain's desire for its racial and religious purity actually triggers off simultaneously both a process of assimilation (if Jews and Arabs consent to religious conversion), and an expulsion (if they refuse), and second, what Anselmo / Spain is doing is defiling and destroying his / its own self as well as the others by placing the other under paranoiac surveillance.

If Lotario is the double of Anselmo, then not only Anselmo, but also Lotario is paranoiac. This can be seen from the way Lotario idealises the body of Camila – first as a diamond, and then as an ermine, as a mirror of glass, as a holy relic not to be touched, as a garden and finally as glass (280–81). This is not only a clear paranoiac regression of the body, a fear about the body, but also a male regulation of the woman's body, which reveals the economics of desire between Anselmo and Lotario (Wilson 1987, 26–7). Camila is now 'mineralized' and turned into currency, functioning as an item of exchange between Anselmo and Lotario. What Lotario is saying is that a woman should be adored but not be touched. Here Lotario is simultaneously speaking for women and voicing his own attitudes towards the body. This expulsion of the other and this repression of his own self and body are like what Anselmo symbolizes – Spanish assimilation and expulsion of Jews and Arabs at the end of the fifteenth century.

In the manuscript of 'The Man Who Was Recklessly Curious', it is the woman who is put to test by the force of paranoid curiosity and madness, and likewise, the manuscript of Don Quixote's history is constructed around Dulcinea, whose enchantment motivates Don Quixote's adventures and is part of his madness. The enchantment of Dulcinea works on two levels, as it can mean both Dulcinea being enchanted and the enchantment by Dulcinea. In the former, Dulcinea is in an object position, being enchanted by some evil spirits as believed by Don Quixote, while in the latter, she is the one who enchants Don Quixote until before his death. In the second sense, Don Quixote is enchanted by Dulcinea, who is good at 'salting pork'. Dulcinea in this sense is implicitly referred to as Circe in Greek mythology. In *The Odyssey*, Homer mentions Circe's power of enchantments, especially in turning Odysseus' men into pigs.[7] Circe is a beautiful yet dangerous witch, skilful in all enchantments but seems to have little love for humankind. She makes Odysseus' companions lose their memory by offering them a drug to drink and then turns them into swine. In *Don Quixote*, Dulcinea's skills in salting pork imply her witchcraft, especially with regard to her enchantment. In other words, Dulcinea may symbolize Circe and may be a witch.

What this foregrounds is the power of the witch, which is enchanting, seductive and destabilizing. This feminine power is enchanting in that it makes one forget his past and lose his memories. It is seductive as not only the characters, but also the reader, are drawn into the text, with a desire to know and to understand, like the narration of Scheherazade in *The Arabian Nights*,[8] in which the female narration,

---

[7] Homer, *The Odyssey*, trans. Robert Fagles, (Harmondsworth: Penguin Books, 1996), Book 10, ll. 252–68 read:

> So he urged and the men called out and hailed her.
> She opened her gleaming doors at once and stepped forth,
> inviting them all in, and in they went, all innocence.
> Only Eurylochus stayed behind – he sensed a trap …
> She ushered them in to sit on high-backed chairs,
> then she mixed them a potion – cheese, barley
> and pale honey mulled in Pramnian wine –
> but into the brew she stirred her wicked drugs
> to wipe from their memories any thought of home.
> Once they'd drained the bowls she filled, suddenly
> she struck with her wand, drove them into her pigsties,
> all of them bristling into swine – with grunts,
> snouts – even their bodies, yes, and only
> the men's minds stayed steadfast as before.
> So off they went to their pens, sobbing, squealing
> as Circe flung them acorns, cornel nuts and mast,
> common fodder for hogs that root and roll in mud.

[8] *Arabian Nights' Entertainments*, ed. Robert L. Mack (Oxford: Oxford University Press, 1995), based on Antoine Galland's 12-volume *Mille et une Nuits* (1704–17), and

circular and mirror-like, has a seductive force to postpone death. The power of the witch in the form of seduction is also destabilizing because of which, narrative, chronological narration and patriarchy are undone. The manuscript can no longer subsume heterogeneous elements into a homogeneous structure, because of its untotalizability. The power of Cervantes is the power of the witch and the power of seduction. It seems that the ultimate, archetypical witch behind his manuscripts is himself, writing in a feminine hand to seduce and bewitch the reader.

This reveals the witchcraft of the manuscript and its seductiveness and power to transform and to destabilize. Reading and interpreting a manuscript is like drinking a love potion that will enchant you, make you lose your memories and subjectivity, and transform your identity.[9] The manuscript is amorphous as it has both liquid and wind qualities – liberating and non-paralyzing qualities. It invites and resists interpretation, effecting encoding and decoding at the same time. Madness is closely related to it as it destroys subjectivity, especially through the power of witch and woman. All these relate to the manuscript found. But what about the manuscript lost?

The manuscript can be regarded not only as a relic of the past, but also as a process of fragmentation, especially when manuscripts are not bound into a book form. Such fragmentation results in non-totalizability. What is destroyed in the process of fragmentation is the totality of the narrative, and the meaning and attributability of the text. In this light, the manuscript is a site in which both fragmentation and destruction are at work. The manuscript is doomed to fall into oblivion and the devouring of both time and human, and if so, Borges's stories can be regarded as a kind of consumptive writing. His short story 'The Garden of Forking Paths' begins with the missing of the first two pages of the statement, which indicates the fragmentary nature of this manuscript. The word 'statement' is strange and it is described as 'dictated, reread, and signed by Dr. Yu Tsun' (119), suggesting it is more like a police confession (Tambling 1991, 80). It remains unexplained why this manuscript of the police confession is incomplete, but it shows the intrigue of a fragmented manuscript.

The manuscript, whether lost or found, embodies the processes of fragmentation and destruction, consumption and oblivion. If the manuscript is non-originating, non-totalizable and anti-patriarchal, its paradoxical status is further heightened as it is housed in the totalizing, paralyzing and patriarchal structure of the archive. The dialectics between the archive and the manuscript seems to fall into an antagonistic existence – the paralyzing archive draws to itself liberating manuscripts while the non-totalizable manuscripts require a totalizing confinement. Their co-existence

---

Tales from the Thousand and One Nights, trans. N.J. Dawood, (Harmondsworth: Penguin Books, 1973). 'Scheherazade' is also spelt as 'Shahrazad' in *The Arabian Nights: Tales from A Thousand and One Nights*, trans. Sir Richard F. Burton (New York: The Modern Library, 2001).

[9] As in Cervantes' 'The Glass Graduate' in *Exemplary Stories*, trans. Lesley Lipson (Oxford: Oxford University Press, 1998), p. 112.

seems to be both mutually repelling and magnetizing. The archive housed with manuscripts is thus a place of its own opposition, a place perpetually out of place, a place of origin containing non-origin and a totality untotalizable.

Like the archive, the concept of the manuscript is not easy to define. Its complexity lies in the fact that it not only refers simply to handwritten records or unbound texts, but it also symbolizes fragmentation, non-origination and non-attributability. In this regard, a book, a chronicle or even memory can also be considered a manuscript metaphorically if it possesses the qualities that the manuscript symbolizes.

Part 2 'Cervantes' Archive' will focus on how this paradoxical interplay between the archive and the manuscript is captured playfully by Cervantes' use of tropelía and bewitchment and by his foregrounding, implicit or explicit, conscious or unconscious, of the destabilizing role of the seducer, female narrator, through his short story 'The Dialogue of the Dogs' and Don Quixote's adventure in the Cave of Montesinos.

PART 2
Cervantes' Archive

Chapter 3
Tropelía and 'The Dialogue of the Dogs'

In *Archive Fever*, Derrida foregrounds the masculinity of the archive by coining the term 'patriarchive' (Derrida 1996, 4). But what is found in the masculine structure of the archive? The answer is: feminine manuscripts, which are liberating and non-totalizable. This nature of the manuscript will be further scrutinized in this chapter through Cervantes' 'The Dialogue of the Dogs', with stress on how tropelía is effected in the manuscript of the dog. The relationship among tropelía, the witch, witchcraft, allegory and utopianism will also be discussed.

What is tropelía? In 'The Dialogue of the Dogs', one of Cervantes' *Exemplary Stories*,[1] when describing the power of the witch Camacha, Cañizares, another witch and Camacha's disciple, claims that:

> As for the stories that are told about the enchantresses of old, who changed men into beasts, those who know most about it claim that it was merely a case of their beauty and charms attracting men so powerfully that they fell madly in love with them. They then kept them in a state of subjection and made them do whatever they wanted, so that they seemed like beasts. But in you, my son, experience is showing me that the contrary is true; I know you are a rational person and I see you in the form of a dog, unless this is being done by means of the art known as *tropelía* which makes one thing appear as another. (283) (original italics)

Tropelía is an art making one thing appear as another, and hence, it is an art confusing appearance and reality. Things and people are not what they appear. In this light, tropelía can be regarded as an art of rhetoric, a language 'characterized by artificial or ostentatious expression' (*OED*), as allegory which does not require compatibility between the signifier and the signified, and as a magical transformation of the reality, a magic realism, which is a 'renegotiation of imagination and reality'.[2] Thomas Hart points out that the concept of tropelía is closely related to the Renaissance idea of the flexibility of the self. He explains that:

---

1 Cervantes, *Exemplary Stories* trans. Lesley Lipson (Oxford and New York: Oxford University Press, 1998), pp. 250–305.

2 Edwin Williamson (ed), 'The Quixotic Roots of Magic Realism: History and Fiction from Alejo Carpentier to Gabriel García Márquez', in *Cervantes and the Modernists: The Question of Influence* (London: Tamesis Books Ltd., 1994), pp. 103–20. The issue to 'allegory' is highly relevant not only to the concept of tropelía, but to 'The Dialogue of the Dogs' as well. This will be discussed in greater detail in Section 3.3.

> In the earlier Renaissance, … flexibility means man's freedom to choose his destiny and to shape himself into an ideal being. A different conception of flexibility, which becomes dominant in the second half of the sixteenth century though it is found earlier in such writers as Machiavelli, stresses rather man's inability to transform himself. The earlier ideal of vertical flexibility gives way to an ideal of lateral resourcefulness, the ability to adapt oneself to changing circumstances.[3]

The history of tropelía reveals its meaning – flexible, changing, transforming. Its connotation changes from a Renaissance ideal of vertical flexibility by which one can transform his own shape or guise into an ideal being to a sixteenth-century ideal of lateral resourcefulness by which he is able to adapt himself to his changing circumstances. It is no coincidence that both meanings of tropelía involve a sense of utopian pursuit of domination – the domination of one's own self (internal or external), a state of self-mastery in order to dominate the external environment. Cervantes in 'The Dialogue of the Dogs' cleverly employs both meanings. What happens to Berganza, in Cañizares' eye, is a vertical flexibility, although not effected by Berganza himself, while Berganza's lateral resourcefulness is manifested through his ease with taking on a new role with each of his new masters.

The witch's power of tropelía generates not only flexibility in terms of bewitchment, transformation, subjection and de-subjectivity, but also a feminine refusal to be stabilized in masculine patriarchal representation and a utopian vision of internal and external domination. In narrative terms, tropelía represents a feminine, destabilizing resistance to and a utopian pursuit of a narrative space in patriarchal discourse, which is manifested in 'The Dialogue of the Dogs' through the presence and the preponderance of the figure of the witch and through the destabilizing nature of the text.

3.1. Non-originating Dialogue

Bewitchment is one of the constant themes of Cervantes, and this, which entails irrationality and magic, is foregrounded in 'The Dialogue of the Dogs'. The story goes as follows: late at night, the two Mahudes' dogs, Scipio and Berganza at the Hospital of the Resurrection, suddenly discover that they enjoy the unprecedented gift of speech. So, Berganza begins to narrate his autobiography – how he shifts from one master to another – a slaughterer, a sheep farmer, a merchant, a constable and a drummer. In the middle of his autobiography is the account of his encounter

---

[3] Thomas R. Hart, 'Renaissance Dialogue Into Novel: Cervantes' Coloquio,' in *MLN*, Vol. 105, No. 2, Hispanic Issue (March 1990), pp. 191–202. In this article and his another article 'Cervantes' Sententious Dogs' (*MLN*, Vol. 94, No. 2, Hispanic Issue (March 1979), 377–86), Hart discusses different roles of the characters in this story in terms of narration, which will be discussed at a later stage in this chapter.

with a witch Cañizares, who claims that she and Berganza's mother, Montiela, learn witchcraft from a famous powerful witch Camacha. She also reveals that actually Berganza is turned into a dog by Camacha out of jealousy by means of tropelía. She promises to turn him back to his human form, but during the process, she is unconscious. Berganza attempts to bring her around by dragging her unconscious naked body out into a courtyard, resulting in her being humiliated by a crowd of onlookers. Hence, Berganza has to run away, and finally stays at the hospital with Scipio.

What further complicates the story is that it is mentioned in the story 'The Deceitful Marriage', which precedes Berganza's autobiography. In 'The Deceitful Marriage', there are stories within stories, lies within lies and deception within deception. This story also unfolds in the form of a dialogue, but this time, it is a dialogue between a syphilitic but convalescing soldier Ensign Campuzano and his friend Graduate Peralta, which symbolizes a dialogue between arms and letters. Ensign Campuzano's story of how he is deceived by deceitful Dona Estefania de Caicedo is also a story of how deceitful he himself is. Campuzano says that he overhears the whole dialogue between the two dogs when he is convalescing at the Hospital of the Resurrection and so he records it to the minute details on a manuscript. The whole dialogue of the dogs unfolds while its 'author' Ensign Campuzano falls asleep. This signifies the lapse of consciousness and rationality and the onset of the irrational and the magical. At the same time, this implies the surrender of authorship and also underlines the destabilization of authorship, the importance of the reader and thus the liberation of meanings.

The figure of this destabilization, liberation and bewitchment is the witch. The witch is a feminine figure standing for a refusal of historicity, especially a refusal to be the creation of patriarchy, and to be represented in patriarchal discourse[4]. Likewise, one salient characteristic of 'The Dialogue of the Dogs' is its non-originating structure, which can be regarded as a refusal to be historicized and a refusal to be stabilized by an origin. This is a refusal to be historicized as the narrative of the life of Berganza is not done through a linear historical fashion, but through interpolating texts. The speech of the witch Cañizares is embedded within Berganza's own narrative, which is embedded in Ensign Campuzano's manuscript. This novella is also a feminine text with a centrally embedded narrative on witches. At the same time, this is a refusal to be stabilized by an origin in that there is simply no origin for the text to originate from. Hence, its beginning is problematized.

But this short story is non-originating in another sense. Its origin is problematized because it has too many beginnings. This is in contrast with Dickens' 'A Madman's Manuscript' (discussed in Chapter 2), in which there are too many conclusions, but a dubious beginning. It seems natural that the story starts with its title and subtitle 'Story and dialogue that took place between Scipio and Berganza, who are commonly known as Mahudes' dogs and who belong to

---

4 See Diane Purkiss, *The Witch in History: Early Modern and Twentieth-century Representations* (London and New York: Routledge, 1996), pp. 2, 11 and 15.

the Hospital of the Resurrection, which is in the city of Valladolid, outside the Campo Gate'. This subtitle is worthy of our attention in two ways. First of all, 'The Dialogue of the Dogs' is the only short story in *Exemplary Stories* that is subtitled in the Oxford edition translated by Lesley Lipson.[5] Second, it is unusual to have such a long subtitle for a short story. The subtitle orientates the reader with details of the genre of the text (a story, a dialogue), the characters (Scipio and Berganza, who are known as Mahudes' dogs) and the locale (the Hospital of the Resurrection, the city of Valladolid, outside the Campo Gate). However, another plausible beginning of this story is at the end of its preceding story 'The Deceitful Marriage'. At the end of his story, Ensign Campuzano mentions Scipio and Berganza:

> The fact is that one night, the night before my final sweat treatment, I heard and as good as saw these two dogs with my own eyes, the one called Scipio and the other Berganza, lying on some old matting behind my bed. In the middle of the night, as I was lying awake in the darkness, thinking about my past affairs and present misfortunes, I heard voices talking close by and I listened very carefully to see whether I could discover who was talking and what they were talking about. I soon realized from the nature of their conversation that it was the two dogs, Scipio and Berganza, who were doing the talking. (247)

This has the same function of the subtitle of 'The Dialogue of the Dogs' as Ensign Campuzano has given details regarding the genre (a dialogue), the protagonists (Scipio and Berganza) and the locale (at the hospital). Fearing that Graduate Peralta does not believe him, the soldier exhibits his manuscript of the whole dialogue of the dogs and lets the Graduate read it when he falls asleep (which echoes 'The Man Who Was Recklessly Curious' in *Don Quixote*, Part 1, Chapters 33–5, which unfolds when Don Quixote is asleep. In both texts, the sleep of the characters signifies both the surrender of authorship and narratorship, and the disappearance of reality):

> The Ensign lay back in his chair, the Graduate opened the notebook, and on the first page he saw the following title – (249)

This is the end of 'The Deceitful Marriage'. But this is not the real ending of this story. The real ending appears at the end of 'The Dialogue of the Dogs':

> The graduate finished reading the dialogue and the ensign woke up at one and the same moment and the graduate said, ' … I appreciate the craftsmanship of the dialogue and its inventiveness, so be satisfied with that. Let's go to the Espolón to exercise our bodies, since I've already exercised my mind.'
>
> 'Let's be off,' said the ensign.
>
> And off they went. (305)

[5] Cervantes, *Exemplary Stories* trans. Lesley Lipson (Oxford and New York: Oxford University Press, 1998).

This shows that first, 'The Deceitful Marriage' actually ends at the end of 'The Dialogue of the Dogs'. Second, 'The Dialogue of the Dogs' is not complete on its own, but is an embedded story within the story of 'The Deceitful Marriage', a narrative interpolated in another one. This technique of narrative embedding is especially dizzying and complex here, and can be regarded as tropelía. In Gérard Genette's terminology, the first framing narrative is called 'extradiegetic' (Genette 1980, 228) and the narrative embedded is called 'metadiegetic' (Genette 1980, 228).[6] Berganza's 'autobiography' falls into a metadiegetic relation to the story written by Campuzano and read by his friend Peralta, which in turn is metadiegetic in relation to that written by Cervantes. Likewise, Berganza's story also embeds the witch Cañizares' story of her life and Berganza's mother's life, which are metadiegetic in relation to Berganza's story.

In such embedding narratives, the narrator of the first narrative becomes the character in his own narrative in the second degree. However, this is problematized here. Berganza is a homodiegetic narrator in that he himself is a character in the story that he narrates. Since it is his autobiography in which he is his narrative's protagonist, his story is an 'autodiegetic narrative' in Genette's terms (Genette 1980, 245). But when Cañizares begins to narrate her story, Berganza becomes neither the narrator nor the protagonist. These roles are now played by Cañizares. Berganza takes on the role of a listener, a narratee, a character to whom the story is told, and his dog-companion Scipio thus becomes a narratee in the second degree. Cañizares' story is therefore an autodiegetic narrative embedded within Berganza's autodiegetic narrative which is embedded within an extradiegetic one, since Campuzano appears in 'The Dialogue of the Dogs' only once, though not by name, when Scipio notices but mistakes that the soldier is asleep and hence will not overhear their dialogue: 'Scipio: No one, I think, although there is a soldier close by undergoing a sweat treatment, but at the moment he will be more inclined to sleep than listen to anyone' (252). In this sense, Campuzano is both an extradiegetic narrator and a second-degree narratee of the story Berganza tells Scipio.[7] Through these embedding narratives, Berganza's biography is told not only by the others, for example, Campuzano and Cañizares, but also by himself. This allows the reader to consider not only his adventures but also the way he

[6] At first glance, it may not seem right for the thing embedded to be 'meta', but Genette explains in the footnote on p. 228 that '[t]he prefix *meta-* obviously connotes here, as in "metalanguage," the transition to the second degree: the *metanarrative* is a narrative within the narrative, the *metadiegesis* is the universe of this second narrative, as the *diegesis* (according to a now widespread usage) designates the universe of the first narrative. We must admit, however, that this term functions in a way opposite to that of its model in logic and linguistics: metalanguage is a language in which one speaks of another language, so metanarrative should be the first narrative, within which one would tell a second narrative. But it seemed to me that it was better to keep the simplest and most common designation for the first degree, and thus to reverse the direction of interlocking. Naturally, the eventual third degree will be a meta-metannarrative, with its meta-metadiegesis, etc.' (original italics)

[7] For more detailed discussion on this, see Thomas R. Hart's 'Cervantes' Sententious Dogs,' *MLN*, Vol. 94, No. 2, Hispanic Issue (March 1979), pp. 377–86.

interprets them, by staging a contrast between his experiences and his own interpretation of his life and adventures. In this regard, telling is interpreting and through the process of telling a tale, the narrator's interpretation inevitably creeps into his own narrative.

Third, the title and the subtitle of 'The Dialogue of the Dogs' do not perform its 'proper' function, that is, to frame or territorialize one narrative from another. These two stories problematize and destabilize the framing and boundary of narrative with the presence of multiple narrators and different levels of narratives. Cervantes here plays with the frame of the text, and what is at work here is tropelía, which confuses and unsettles the framing and the territorialization of the text.

3.2. Discourse of a Witch

'The Dialogue of the Dogs' is not only an autobiography of a dog, but also about the witch Cañizares. The story concerns Berganza's recounting of his life and history, after he and Scipio suddenly discover they have the ability of speech, by which their 'speaking goes beyond the bounds of nature' (250). They regard this as a miracle as they can speak coherently and are capable of reason. In this autobiography of Berganza, what is foregrounded is the master-servant structure recast several times. Berganza's first master is a slaughterer named Nicholas Snub-Nose, followed by a sheep farmer, a merchant, a constable and a drummer. In a word, the fundamental structure of Berganza's autobiography is patriarchal in nature – a narrative structured around the master-slave relationship that Berganza has experienced. Each master that he serves consolidates his servitude in the patriarchal structure. In such a patriarchal structure, Berganza is a subject / object handed over from one master to another, from one domination to another, in which the female voice is either marginalized or silenced. Berganza and Scipio believe that dogs are highly commended because of their good memory, gratitude and great fidelity and most importantly because they represent the symbol of friendship (250). These qualities are especially important in the patriarchal master-servant structure and are assumed to be possessed by the servant. The dog, in this regard, is an ideal manifestation of subjection within patriarchy.

Under such subjection within patriarchy, Berganza attempts to narrate his autobiography in a linear fashion:

> *Berganza.* … but now that I remember what I should have said at the beginning of our conversation, not only am I not amazed at what I'm saying, I'm astonished at what I leave unsaid.
>
> *Scipio.* So you can't tell me what you remember now?
>
> *Berganza.* It's a certain incident which took place when I was with a great witch, a disciple of Camacha of Montilla.
>
> *Scipio.* Then tell me what happened before you carry on with your life story.

> *Berganza.* I'll do no such thing until the proper time; be patient, and listen to my adventures in the order in which they took place, for you'll enjoy them more that way, unless your desire to know the middle before the beginning vexes you. (258)

Berganza is a special narrator in that he realizes what is unsaid in a text or narrative is far more significant than what is said. However, he also knows it is not 'proper' to digress in his narration and Scipio takes great pains to pull him back to his autobiographical account. His attempt to narrate in a linear fashion reveals that both Berganza and Scipio are within the grip of patriarchy and ideology as they believe the proper way to narrate is to do it in accordance with temporal linearity in which the middle should not precede the beginning. In this linearity, it is improper to displace times, places and events. This implies that patriarchy has no place for tropelía.

Within such a linear structure of Berganza's autobiography, there is a long speech of the old witch Cañizares, who claims that Berganza's real identity is Montiel, the son of another witch called Montiela, who with Cañizares learns witchcraft from a famous witch called Camacha of Montilla. She explains to Berganza that he is now a dog because when his mother Montiel gave birth to him, Camacha of Montilla, envious of Montiel's growing power and knowledge, turned him into a dog. Cañizares tells Berganza how powerful Camacha is:

> She was so unique [sic] within her profession that the Ericthos, Circes, and Medeas, of whom I've heard that the history books are full could not rival her. She'd freeze the clouds at will, covering the face of the sun with them, and when she felt like it she would calm the stormiest sky. In an instant she'd bring men from distant lands; she'd wondrously repair young ladies who had been careless in guarding their integrity; she provided a cover of modesty for immodest widows; she annulled and arranged marriages as she pleased. In December she had fresh roses in her garden and in January she harvested wheat. (283)

This witch's power is so mighty that she can go against nature – growing roses in December and harvesting wheat in January; calming a stormy sky, and freezing the clouds so as to cover the sun. She is not confined by any spatial territory as she can transport men and bring them from distant lands. As against patriarchy, she is on the side of the females, repairing young ladies careless in guarding their integrity, providing modesty for immodest widows, and annulling and arranging marriages as she pleases. In this respect, she is like Rojas' Celestina, who is an old woman, a go-between and a healer of virgins, giving advice to young lovers, especially to Calisto, who falls in love with Melibea. Celestina tries to bring people together by using her magic and by using her 'slick' language to convince them they should be together.[8] But Camacha is more powerful than Celestina.

---

[8] Fernando de Rojas, *Celestina* trans. James Mabbe (Warminster: Aris and Phillips Ltd., 1987), first published in 1499. For more details on Rojas' influence on Cervantes, see "Rojas' Celestina and Cervantes' Cañizares," by Patricia S. Finch, *Cervantes: Bulletin of the Cervantes Society of America*, Vol. 9, No. 2 (1989), pp. 55–62.

She is even mightier than Erictho, Circes and Medea, who are all witches. Like Circes, Camacha can effect bodily changes:

> It was claimed that she could change men into animals and that she'd made use of a sacristan in the form of an ass for six years, really and truly, but I've never been able to figure out how it's done. As for the stories that are told about the enchantresses of old, who changed men into beasts, those who know most about it claim that it was merely a case of their beauty and charms attracting men so powerfully that they fell madly in love with them. They then kept them in a state of subjection and made them do whatever they wanted, so that they seemed like beasts. (283)

Like Circes, Camacha is a beautiful but dangerous witch, with the ability to turn men into beasts, and with her beauty to keep them in a state of subjection. This process of subjection results in de-subjectivity of men in which their taken-for-granted patriarchal status is replaced with a beastly one. In this sense, what Camacha and Circes are doing is not much different from the workings of ideology, patriarchy and colonialism. All of them take away their subject's subjectivity and replace it with a beastly subjection. The only difference lies in the fact that the latter ones very often resort to coercion and hegemony, while the former ones draw their subject towards them through seduction. In other words, there are two kinds of subjection – a masculine one and a feminine one. Tropelía of the witch in this sense belongs to the power of subjection by the female by seduction.

On another level, witchcraft symbolizes a reaction against the power of Western science, which very often stresses a conceptual cause-effect rationality. Keith Thomas claims that the category of the 'witch' was first created in the Renaissance and that its ideological function is a reaction to the fear of the imperial Western science[9]. In this sense, science is masculine, encountered by witchcraft as feminine. What witchcraft accentuates is the irrational, sexual and magical, through which patriarchy is further destabilized. The central motifs of 'The Dialogue of the Dogs' in this light are 'witches', 'source of witches' magic' and 'evil deeds of witches'.[10] More importantly, this reveals that tropelía and witchcraft work in a similar fashion.

3.3. Allegory and Utopianism

This destabilizing witch upsetting the order and authority of patriarchy and ideology through seduction may reveal another aspect of Cervantes'

[9] Keith Thomas, *Religion and the Decline of Magic* (New York: Scribner's Sons, 1971), especially Chapter 16, 'The Making of a Witch' and Chapter 17, 'Witchcraft and its Social Environment'.

[10] See Terence L. Hansen, 'Folk Narrative Motifs, Beliefs, and Proverbs in Cervantes' *Exemplary Novels*' in *The Journal of American Folklore*, Vol. 72, No. 283 (January–March 1959), pp. 24–9.

deterritorializing writing.[11] Within the linear text of Berganza's autobiography, what Cañizares has said about Camacha, Montiela and herself can be regarded as allegorical. After listening to Berganza's account of Cañizares' speech, Scipio says:

> ... what must appear to you like prophecies are nothing but fairy stories and old wives' tales, like the ones about the headless horse or the magic wand, with which people entertain themselves round the fireside on long winter nights. It this were not the case, it would have come to pass, unless the words are meant to be taken in a sense I've heard called allegorical, where the meaning is not what the words literally say, but something which, although different, may be similar. (292)

Unlike symbolism in which there is compatibility between the two fragments in order to form a whole, allegory does not require such compatibility. Instead, what is at work is the displacement between these two fragments because of which a totality of meaning will never result. In Paul de Man's terms in 'The Rhetoric of Temporality', 'allegory designates primarily a distance in relation to its own origin, and, renouncing the nostalgia and the desire to coincide, it establishes its language in the void of this temporal difference' (de Man 1983, 207). It is through such displacement of fragments and such temporal difference that allegory is destabilizing. As Angus Fletcher points out, allegory says one thing and means another: 'It destroys the normal expectation we have about language, that our words "mean what they say." When we predicate quality *x* of person Y, Y really is what our predication says he is (or we assume so); but allegory would turn Y into something other (*allos*) than what the open and direct statement tells the reader' (Fletcher 1964, 2). Benjamin in *The Origin of German Tragic Drama* says allegory is the art of the fragment in which meaning breaks down and possibility of transmitting meaning is in vain (Benjamin 1998, 116 and 176). If the whole Cañizares' speech on witches and witchcraft as well as Berganza's mother can only be encoded in the form of allegorical writing, this can be regarded as tropelía, destabilizing patriarchy and ideology.

In this story, the destabilization is doubled – it is manifested through a speech of a witch who is a marginalized female figure in patriarchy, and at the same time, the speech is in the form of allegory. This story can also be regarded as a critique of the genre of (auto)biography in that this autobiography of Berganza comes in three forms. First, Berganza himself narrates most of his life, his different masters and adventures; second another version of his life is narrated by a destabilizing witch in an allegorical discourse; and third, the whole text of this autobiography

---

[11] See *Cervantes and the Mystery of Lawlessness: A Study of El casamiento engañoso y El coloquio de los perros*, by Alban K. Forcione (New Jersey: Princeton University Press, 1984), especially pp. 72–88, which focus on the images of tomb, confinement, physical infirmity, mutilation and the like to prove that Cervantes is writing in 'a grammar of narrative disorder'.

is transcribed by Ensign Campuzano in the preceding story. Of course, there is the invisible hand of Cervantes behind these three versions. This fits well into the etymological meaning of 'allegory', which means 'other' (*allos*) and 'speaking out the market place' (*agoreuein*) (*OED*). This autobiography of Berganza is hybrid and heterogeneous in nature, in which meaning is allegorical and destabilized. When he tells of his own life and history, it is inevitable that he speaks of the others, and ironically and inversely, his own biography is not told by himself only, but also by others like Cañizares and Ensign Campuzano. This inversibility itself is part of the workings of allegory as allegory can also be defined as a figure of inversion.[12] An autobiography in this light is not a monophonic account of one's life and more importantly, that it may be an account narrated by somebody else. If so, an autobiography can never be *auto*biography, but *allo*biography.

One peculiar aspect of the three destabilizing, wicked witches in 'The Dialogue of the Dogs' is their implicit utopianism. Before Montiela dies, Camacha says to her:

> They will resume their proper guise
> When they observe with their own eyes
> The arrogant laid low,
> The meek raised to the skies,
> By a hand empower'd to do so. (285)

This is a utopian vision that Camacha predicts, that Montiela puts in black and write and that Cañizares commits to memory. 'Their proper guise' refers to the dogs' proper 'shape'. This raises the issues of what a 'proper' guise / shape is (and what is not) on the one hand, and the vanishing distinction between 'guise' and 'shape' on the other. If the bodily shape is only a guise, a false appearance, or a mode of dress, this further problematizes the concept of identity and suggests all identity is only a form of a guise or a mask. Tropelía in this regard is a utopian pursuit in which the guise, shape or appearance is never fixed.

In such a utopian vision of the moment when Berganza and his unknown brother 'resume their proper guise', what is predicted is a carnivalesque world in which the arrogant and the meek are displaced, reverse and inverse: 'the arrogant laid low, the meek raised to the skies'. This utopian vision echoes the one found in the Bible:

> He hath shewed strength with his arm; he hath scattered the proud in the imagination of their hearts.

---

[12] Suggested by Fletcher in *Allegory: The Theory of a Symbolic Mode*, p. 2n1, quoting Thomas Elyot and Edward Phillips:

> 'e.g. ed. Thomas Cooper, in Thomas Elyot, *Bibliotheca Eliotae: Eliotes Dictionarie* (London, 1559): "*Allegoria* – a figure called inversion, where it is one in woordes, and an other in sentence or meaning"; Edward Phillips, in *The New World of English Words* (4th ed., London, 1678): "*Allegory* – Inversion or changing: In Rhetorick it is a mysterious saying, wherein there is couched something that is different from the literal sense."

> He hath put down the mighty from their seats, and exalted them of low degree. He hath filled the hungry with good things; and the rich he hath sent empty away.
>
> (The Gospel According to Luke, 1.51–3, King James Version)

Conceivably this utopian world of carnivalesque displacement and inversion is most appropriate to be expressed in the form of allegory. But this utopian moment is attainable only by a 'hand' empowered to effect such tropelía and inversion. This hand is allegorical and it can refer to another witch, God, fate, writer or even Cervantes as the whole story flows out of the pen held in his hand on the manuscript of this story. Scipio tries to decode the meaning of these five lines:

> it seems to me to mean that we'll recover our form when we see that those who were yesterday at the top of the wheel of fortune are today humbled and laid low at the feet of misfortune and despised by those who held them in highest esteem. Similarly, when we see that those who a couple of hours ago had no other role to play in the world than increase the number of its inhabitants, are now raised so high by good fortune that we've lost sight of them. If at first we couldn't see them because they were so small and timid, now we can't touch them because they are so great and exalted. If recovering the form you mention were dependent on this, we've already seen it happen and it happens all the time; which leads me to deduce that it's not in the allegorical sense, but in the literal that Camacha's words are to be understood. (292)

Scipio rejects Camacha's utopian vision, claiming that the reversal of the arrogant and the meek has been seen and that it happens all the time. Thus, he refuses to take Camacha's words allegorically, but reads them literally. He does not believe Camacha, saying that 'Camacha was a lying trickster, Cañizares a rascal, and Montiela a malicious and wicked fool, begging your pardon, in case she's the mother of both of us, or yours alone, for I don't want her for a mother' (293). By refusing to read Camacha's lines allegorically, he at the same time denies that they are witches and thinks that they are only tricksters, rascals and fools. This also reveals his implicit rejection of Berganza's account of his autobiography. He puts Berganza's autobiography and Cañizares' account in doubt by first pointing out Camacha's lines can be read allegorically (292) and then refuting this immediately (292–3). But when he comes to unpack what this 'hand' signifies, he ironically speaks in an allegorical discourse:

> I declare, then, that the true meaning's a game of ninepin bowling, where the pins that are standing are promptly knocked down and raised again by a hand with the skill to do it. Think, then, whether over the course of our lives we've ever witnessed a game of ninepins and if as a result of it we've turned into men, if that's what we are. (293)

Their lives are regarded allegorically as a game of ninepin bowling and thus their ups and downs are like the pins being knocked down and raised again by a hand playing such a game. Scipio tries to de-allegorize these lines allegorically and his allegorical reading of these lines, whether they are allegorical or not, only results in intensifying their allegorical nature. Interpretation, after all, is a kind of translation, which according to Fletcher is inversion in an allegorical sense.[13] In this regard, Scipio's interpretation has already turned Camacha's lines into allegory although he himself denies their allegorical nature. This suggests the allegorical nature of every interpretation and translation. This also reveals that allegory is tropelía.

All the destabilization and bewitchment of the witch discussed above can be summarized in terms of tropelía. In Cervantes' text, this confusion of the appearance and the reality made through the figure of the witch. It is through such a bewitching figure that imagination and reality are re-negotiated, resulting in a liberating, flexible and magically transforming world. This tropelía, manifesting itself in the forms of allegory and utopianism, can also be regarded as the force behind 'The Dialogue of the Dogs'. In this regard, this short story is a text of tropelía. This is a manuscript of tropelía, which is destabilizing, transforming and non-totalizable. The world created out of tropelía is not only liberating and flexible, but also utopian. This chapter focuses on one of Cervantes' texts only, but what it reveals is an important footing and an obsessive theme for writers in Cervantes' shadows, like Borges, Puig and García Márquez. For them, this world of tropelía is an archive offered by Cervantes. In this regard, the concept of the archive can be expanded to mean not simply a collection of manuscripts or books, but a single text which draws the others towards it. Hence, Cervantes' archive is defined not by the quantity of his works stored or the spatial presence of a library for such a purpose, but by the effects of his writing upon the others, the scope of his 'shadow'. How Cervantes' archive is visited and raided by these writers will be discussed in Part 3, but before that, let's look at this archive in relation to tropelía, Don Quixote and his knight-errantry in the next chapter.

---

[13] Fletcher, *Allegory: The Theory of a Symbolic Mode* p. 2n1: 'Sometimes the term *inversio* may be taken in its original sense of *translation*, ...'

Chapter 4
Descent into Tropelía: Don Quixote in the Cave

While in 'The Dialogue of the Dogs', tropelía comes through the figure of a bewitching witch, in Don Quixote's adventure in the Cave of Montesinos (Part 2, Chapters 22–4 of *Don Quixote*), it manifests itself as Don Quxiote's response to Sancho Panza's trick on him in Part 2, Chapter 10, and his account of what he experiences in his adventures in the cave can be regarded as an example of tropelía, through which Don Quixote takes his revenge for Sancho Panza's trick on him. In this chapter, the tropelía that Don Quixote experiences in the cave will be discussed to unravel its destabilization of the binary opposites of inside / outside, real / unreal and life / death. A Lacanian reading of this cave episode is offered by Sullivan, but will be contested to show that Don Quixote's utopian adventures and knight-errantry can be regarded as tropelía for creating a past for a better future.

4.1. Tropelía in the Cave

'The Dialogue of the Dogs' and *Don Quixote* share a number of similarities. The companionship between Berganza and Scipio with the presence of a witch can be comparable to the knight-squire relationship between Don Quixote and Sancho Panza with the presence of the allegedly bewitched Dulcinea. Moreover, tropelía is manifested in *Don Quixote* not in terms of vertical flexibility, but in terms of lateral resourcefulness. Don Quixote's credo is 'I know who I am and I know I can be not only those I have mentioned, but the Twelve Peers of France as well, and even all the nine paragons of Fame, for my deeds will surpass all those they performed, together or singly' (43). In short, his credo is – I know who I am and can be everybody. Adroit improvisation is made not only by Don Quixote, but also by Sancho Panza, especially his successful attempt in Part 2, Chapter 10 to convince Don Quixote that the three peasant girls they encounter are Dulcinea and her two maids, which makes Don Quixote believe that an evil enchanter has prevented him from seeing his lady as who she really is. To Don Quixote, this is a situation of tropelía – a confusion of reality and appearance.

As with 'The Dialogue of the Dogs', an allegorical utopian pursuit is strong in *Don Quixote*. José Antonio Maravall points out that during the period when *Don Quixote* was written, Cervantes was immersed with a utopian dream of an ideal Spain, especially after experiencing a period of tension between hopes and disappointments, beliefs and doubts, likes and dislikes (Maravall 1991, 25–6). Cervantes' lifetime experienced the climax and the decline of Spain's golden age. Between 1529, the year of the reign of Charles V, and 1605, when the first part of *Don Quixote* was published and when Philip III was still presiding over the extensive Spanish dominions, imperial dignity and the Spanish monarchy were separated. Once Spain was proud of her achievements in subduing the populations in the New World, which was a source of treasure that supported the military might of Charles V and Philip II, but the defense of Spain exhausted the resources of her own land and that of her colonies, and after the defeat of the Armada in 1588, the country was too impoverished to recover. Maravall believes that Cervantes, when writing *Don Quixote*, was overwhelmed by a melancholic sympathy with the ideal connected with the great spiritual movement of preceding generations, as well as by a sad recognition of the impossibility of realizing this ideal (Maravall 1991, 26). If *Don Quixote* is read in this light, Don Quixote's adventures are not simply mad or romantic, but actually utopian in nature. What Don Quixote represents is a spirit of humanistic utopianism in the early modern world in the seventeenth century.

Don Quixote's strange adventure in the Cave of Montesinos is an experience of tropelía in which it is undecidable whether Don Quixote is awake or dreaming and whether he is lying or telling the truth. After spending three days with the newlyweds (Basilio and Quiteria), Don Quixote departs for the supposedly enchanted Cave of Montesinos with Sancho Panza and one of Basilio's student friends as guide. He clears the entrance, ties a rope 60 feet long around his waist and descends into the cave. After half an hour, the scholar and Sancho Panza pull on the rope but find no weight on it. Out of panic, Sancho hauls in the line as fast as he can and finally they draw Don Quixote onto the ground. Don Quixote opens his eyes, as if awakening from a deep sleep. After a meal, Don Quixote relates to them his adventures in the cave. In his cave, Don Quixote finds himself in a castle where he meets the knight Sir Montesinos, who shows him the body of Durandarte, one of the greatest knights-errant in history. Durandarte's last wish before he had been killed was that his heart be cut out and given to his Belerma. Don Quixote learns that because of the curse of a wicked enchanter, Durandarte cannot really die, and that Belerma too is cursed with immortality and has become an old ugly lady who wanders around carrying Durandarte's heart. Then, Don Quixote sees three peasant girls that Sancho had told him of (in Part 2, Chapter 10). They are Dulcinea and her two ladies-in-waiting. One of the ladies comes to Don Quixote and asks him to lend Dulcinea six reales, which stuns Don Quixote. However, Don Quixote can only give her four. When he hands over the money to her, Sancho hauls him out of the cave and he wakes up.

This cave episode is of a strange status in *Don Quixote* especially regarding its authenticity. Even the alleged author of this text, Cide Hamete Benengeli is not sure about the authenticity of this adventure and writes in his own hand in the margin of his manuscript:

> I cannot believe, nor can I persuade myself, that everything written in the preceding chapter actually happened in its entirety to the valiant Don Quixote: the reason is that all the adventures up to this point have been possible and plausible, but with regard to this one in the cave, I can find no way to consider it true since it goes so far beyond the limits of reason. (Part 2, Chapter 24, 614)

The whole cave episode comes in the form of interpolation. This interpolation is at odds with the flow of the plot, interrupting the preceding (Don Quixote as peacemaker and the wedding of Camacho and Quiteria, Part 2, Chapters 19–21) and subsequent parts (The Adventure of the Puppeteer, Part 2, Chapters 25–7) of the novel. This interpolation and disjunction add to the effect of tropelía. Nobody is sure whether Don Quixote is lying or telling the truth regarding what he has experienced inside the cave. Even Sancho Panza is in doubt about this and thus asks Master Pedro's fortune-telling ape if what happens in the Cave of Montesinos is true, saying that 'in my opinion, begging your grace's pardon, it was all deception and lies, or at least nothing but dreams' (Part 2, Chapter 25, 627). Cide Hamete Benengeli, who claims to be the author of this part of *Don Quixote* in the Toledo manuscript, further comments that:

> But it is not possible for me to think that Don Quixote, the truest and most noble knight of his day, would lie, for he would not tell a lie even if he were shot with arrows. Moreover, he recounted and told it in all its circumstances and details, and in so short a time he could not fabricate so enormous a quantity of nonsense; if this adventure seems apocryphal, the fault is not mine, and so, without affirming either its falsity or its truth, I write it down. You, reader, since you are a discerning person, must judge it according to your own lights, for I must not and cannot do more; yet it is considered true that at the time of Don Quixote's passing and death, he is said to have retracted it, saying he had invented it because he thought it was consonant and compatible with the adventures he had read in his histories. (Part 2, Chapter 24, 614)

The plurality of authorship of this text has already destabilized the authenticity of the text. Now Cide Hamete Benengeli claims that it is not probable that Don Quixote fabricates what he says to have experienced inside the cave, but at the same time, this alleged author refuses to affirm that it is true, and renounces his responsibility for this, leaving the reader to judge and decide the credibility of Don Quixote's narrative. In other words, the text is left undecidable as its authenticity is destabilized, leading to the same tropelía of Don Quixote's other adventures. However, it is also undecidable whether Cide Hamete Benengeli or Cervantes is mocking the reader when the question of authenticity is cast on a fictional text and when the reader is urged to look into the authenticity of a fictional text.

In the cave of Montesinos, Don Quixote experiences destabilization and displacement. At the outset, his own adventure inside the cave is taken when he falls asleep (which is similar to the unfolding of 'The Dialogue of the Dogs' when Ensign Campuzano falls asleep, and the unfolding of 'The Man Who Was Recklessly Curious' when Don Quixote is asleep). In other words, his adventure in the cave is also an adventure within a dream. Freud claims that a dream is the fulfillment of a wish (*The Interpretation of Dreams*, Chapter 3), but in Don Quixote's dream inside the cave, his wish is not fulfilled. Dulcinea del Toboso in his dream is still enchanted. And a damsel tells Don Quixote that Dulcinea wants to borrow six reales from him, but he can offer only four. When the damsel takes the four reales, she suddenly leaps 5 feet into the air (Part 2, Chapter 23, 613). A Lacanian reading of the six reales has been suggested by Henry W. Sullivan, which goes as follows:

> 0 refers to the pre-mirror stage, when the infant's universe is boundaryless and composed of fragments (that is, pre-mirror boundarylessness)
>
> 1 is the number of the illusory symbiosis of infant and mother in the mirror stage itself (that is, mirror-stage mastery and illusory symbiosis)
>
> 2 is the reality of the split subject, separated and alienated in language by the castrating action of the phallic signifier (that is, post-mirror phallic division)
>
> 3 refers to the Oedipal quality expressed by the Name-of-the-Father, which alone gives meaning to the division of one into two by three and so forms the fundamental triangle of Imaginary relations (that is, Oedipal myth)
>
> 4 means the beginning of a recursion of the Oedipal triangle through exogamy, or marriage outside the clan (that is, exogamy)
>
> 5 is reached upon the birth of children and the reconstitution of the triangle, but with the subject now at a different corner of the triangle, in the role of a parent (that is, paternity / maternity)
>
> 6 refigures this again when children are born to the children of the subject, resulting in perpetuity of lineage (that is, perpetuity) (Sullivan 1996, 129–31)

Sullivan takes the view that when Dulcinea wants to borrow six reales from Don Quixote, she actually asks for perpetuity and wishes to bear Don Quixote's children, but he can only offer four reales, meaning that what he can offer is exogamy / marriage, but not children or grandchildren. Don Quixote's act of entering the cave allegorizes a process of regression, a desire to return to his mother's womb, a journey seeking truth in darkness, or an Odyssey into the unconscious. What Sullivan suggests is Don Quixote's desire to marry Dulcinea. But does Don Quixote really want to marry Dulcinea? Does the 'four reales' really mean marriage? Don Quixote's desire for Dulcinea by no means entails his desire for marriage. Carroll Johnson reads Don Quixote as a person with 'chronic inability to interact successfully with women' and believes that he has an unconscious passion for his niece Sobrina, who is 'lurking at the latent level' of the Cave of Montesinos' adventure (Johnson 1983, 158 and 167). The real object of Don Quixote's desire is his niece, not Dulcinea.[1] In this light, Don Quixote's dream and adventure in the cave can be regarded as his attempt for his repressed desire. Johnson further comments that Don Quixote's failure to produce the requested six reales signifies his 'fear of impotence' as sex is linked with the discourse of debt (Johnson 1983, 158). Moreover, Don Quixote's adventure in the Cave reveals more the dialectic between

---

[1] Ruth Anthony El Saffar and Diana de Armas Wilson believe that it is 'Sobrina' who 'permitted the constitution of new theories: she energized a whole new generation of readers who were curious about the connections between obsessive reading and the operations of desire, including the desire to give dreams meaning.' in *Quixote Desire: Psychoanalytic Perspectives on Cervantes* (Ithaca, NY: Cornell University Press, 1993), p. 71.

reality and dream, disenchantment and bewitchment, mundane existence and a utopian pursuit, than Don Quixote's desire to marry Dulcinea or Dulcinea's desire to bear his children.[2]

One reason that Don Quixote fails to disenchant Dulcinea may be that, instead of being the enchanted, Dulcinea is the enchanter. Earlier on, Don Quixote recounts that Sir Montesinos shows him three village girls:

> … Montesinos showed me three peasant girls who were leaping and jumping in those pleasant fields like nanny goats, and as soon as I saw them I recognized one of them as the peerless Dulcinea of Toboso … (Part 2, Chapter 23, 611)

Dulcinea and her maids appear in front of Don Quixote as if they were three nanny goats leaping and frolicking in the meadows. But the 'goat' can also be the form that the devil is supposed to assume on the witches' sabbath.[3] In 'The Dialogue of the Dogs', Cañizares confesses that

> Many times I've wanted to ask my goat how your affair will end, but I've never dared because he never gives a straight answer to the questions we ask him, but replies in riddles with many possible meanings. So there's no point in asking this lord and master of ours anything, for he mixes a single truth with a thousand lies; and from what I can gather from his replies, he knows nothing about the future with any certainty, only by guesswork. All the same, he's got us witches so fooled, that although he plays lots of tricks on us we can't leave him. (285)

Behind the three witches in 'The Dialogue of the Dogs', there is a more powerful devil in the form of a goat, and this goat is the source of truth which goes together with lies. His language and answers are never direct, but allegorical and in the form of riddles. This embodiment of the devil in the form of a goat can also be found in Albrecht Dürer's engraving 'The Knight, Death and Devil'. In the engraving, the devil is represented in the form of a goat with a swine-snout and a pair of antlers, sneaking behind a heavily armoured knight.[4] Now in the cave of Montesinos, Dulcinea and her two maids come before Don Quixote as if goats. This may imply

---

[2] Analyses on this cave episode have been plentiful. See *The Chivalric World of Don Quijote: Style, Structure, and Narrative Technique* by Howard Mancing (Columbia: University of Missouri Press, 1982), p. 147; *Cervantes and the Mystery of Lawlessness: A Study of El casamiento engañoso y El coloquio de los perros* by Alban K. Forcione (Princeton, NJ: Princeton University Press, 1984), p. 55; *Quixotic Desire: Psychoanalytic Perspectives on Cervantes* ed. Ruth Anthony El Saffar and Diana de Armas Wilson (Ithaca, New York: Cornell University Press, 1993), pp. 70–80; and *Grotesque Purgatory: A Study of Cervantes's Don Quixote, Part II* by Henry W. Sullivan (University Park, PA: The Pennsylvania State University Press, 1996), pp. 30–48.

[3] From Lesley Lipson's footnote to 'The Dialogue of the Dogs' in Cervantes' *Exemplary Stories*, p. 316.

[4] For more details, see *The Life and Art of Albrecht Dürer* by Erwin Panofsky (Princeton, NJ: Princeton University Press, 1955), pp. 151–4.

that she is not really the enchanted, but the enchanter or the witch like those three in 'The Dialogue of the Dogs', or she is the devil whom Cañizares hopes to seek truth from. For Nietzsche,

> Perhaps truth is a woman who has reasons for not letting us see her reasons? Perhaps her name is – to speak Greek – Baubo? (Nietzsche 1974, 38)

And Derrida in *Spurs: Nietzsche's Styles* comments on this, saying that

> Nietzsche revives that barely allegorical figure (of woman) of his own interest. For him, truth is like a woman. It resembles the veiled movement of feminine modesty. Their complicity, the complicity (rather than the unity) between woman, life, seduction, modesty – all the veiled and veiling effects (*Schleier, Enthülung, Verhüllung*) – is developed in a rarely quoted fragment of Nietzsche's. (Derrida 1978, 51) (original italics and bracketing)

First, when truth is like a woman, she is turned into an allegorical figure. Second, veiled and veiling effects are in part generated by her seductive power. But in both 'The Dialogue of the Dogs' and Don Quixote's adventure in the Cave of Montesinos, the woman is the embodiment of not only seduction and truth, but also a witch, a devil and a master of allegorical language mixing and veiling truth with lies. To put this in the context of tropelía, the veiled and veiling illusions from the seductive witch in the form of allegory are what tropelía refers to. Through tropelía, truth and lies are confused, like the confusion between appearance and reality.

But the three ladies Don Quixote encounters in the cave are internalized figures of the three peasant girls Sancho Panza describes in Part 2, Chapter 10 (516–19), one of which is 'round-faced and snub-nosed' (518), who makes Don Quixote dare not open his mouth. Erich Auerbach says that this incident is 'the climax of his [Don Quixote] illusion and disillusionment' (Auerbach 1953, 339) in that Sancho Panza has become more 'quixotic' than his master. Instead of preventing his master's absurdities, Sancho now improvises a scene in the fashion of chivalry through tropelía while 'Don Quijote's ability to transform events to harmonize with his illusion breaks down before the crude vulgarity of the sight of the peasant women' (Auerbach 1953, 339). In this temporary moment, the knight and the squire change roles. The ladies that Don Quixote 'encounters' in the cave can be regarded as the products after his internalizing this event, internalizing what Sancho has said to him about bewitchment. When seeing the ladies in the cave, Don Quixote is thinking in terms of bewitchment and tropelía, not beauty. Hence, Belerma is now an ugly old withered hag. It is no wonder that Don Quixote fails to disenchant Dulcinea, as in his dream fantasy, he has already accepted fiction as truth. What is fictional has already been internalized before he enters the cave. Before his adventure in the cave, Don Quixote has already been in the grip of tropelía, and ironically, this grip of tropelía is from his squire, Sancho Panza, not from a witch.

The tropelía experienced by Don Quixote can be found not only through the destabilization within his dream, but also through the paradoxical displacements during his adventure of the cave. He claims he is wide awake but he falls asleep during his catabasis, a sense of sleeplessness within a sleep. Hence, it is undecidable whether he is within or outside a dream. He is deep inside the cave or dream and hence, far from the waking reality outside the cave. At the same time, it is not unreality that he is experiencing since his utopian mission of fighting against bewitchment carries on in his dream. Rather he is situated in a space of tropelía in which the world is neither real nor unreal and hence the distinction between reality and unreality collapses. It is also in such a space of tropelía that the distinction between life and death is problematized. Inside the cave, when Don Quixote reaches Sir Montesinos' castle, he is introduced to Durandarte. It is odd that he is introduced to somebody who is supposed to be dead, but not quite:

> 'This is my friend Durandarte, the flower and model of enamored and valiant knights of his time; here he lies, enchanted, as I and many others are enchanted, by Merlin, that French enchanter who was, people say, the son of the devil; … What astonishes me is that I know, as well as I know that it is day, that Durandarte ended the days of his life in my arms, and that when he was dead I removed his heart with my own hands; … if this knight really died, why does he now moan and sigh from time to time, as if he were alive?' (Part 2, Chapter 23, 606–7)

Durandarte, instead of dying a peaceful death, weeps and moans on his mortuary slab, begging to be released from the burden of life, as if he were still alive. Likewise, Durandarte's beloved, Belerma, is also a liminal figure between life and death:

> I [Don Quixote] turned my head and saw through the crystal walls a procession of two lines of beautiful maidens passing through another chamber, all of them dressed in mourning and wearing white turbans on their heads, in the Turkish fashion. At the very end and conclusion of the two lines came a matron, for her gravity made her seem one, also dressed in black, and wearing a white train so lengthy and long it brushed the ground. Her turban was twice as large as the largest of the others; she was beetle-browed and snub-nosed; her mouth was large, but her lips were red; her teeth, which she may have shown, were few in number and crooked, though as white as peeled almonds; in her hands she carried a delicate cloth, and in it, … was a heart that had been mummified, it looked so dry and shriveled. (Part 2, Chapter 23, 608–9)

The once beautiful Belerma, now an ugly old woman, wanders around carrying her knight's heart. The knight's heart becomes dry, shrivelled and mummified. The heroic knights and lovely ladies in chivalrous romances now become abject zombies, enchanted and situated in the tropelía of the cave. Even the enchanter Merlin is displaced. He is no longer the Arthurian enchanter, but is displaced from Wales to France and then to Spain.[5]

[5] John Rutherford suggests in his footnotes (Penguin edition, 2001, p. 1011) that Merlin now becomes French because the Arthurian legends came to Spain through France.

Likewise, there is a spatial displacement and the collapse of binary opposites of inside-outside. He is inside the cave but at the same time he finds himself out in a meadow, which means that there is an outside space inside the cave. In terms of temporal displacement, there is a regression during this catabasis. Outside the cave, Sancho Panza experiences a period of half an hour (Part 2, Chapter 22, 603), but inside the cave, Don Quixote first feels it is 'a little more than an hour' (610), and then he thinks three days has passed (610), and later on, he reaches Sir Montesinos' castle in which five hundred years have passed but none of the people there has died.

4.2. Don Quixote and Plato: Two Allegorical Caves

It is obvious that these displacements and destabilization of tropelía experienced in the allegorical cave of Montesinos share similarities with as well as differences from the allegorical cave Plato mentions in Book 7 of *The Republic*. In Plato's cave, men have been prisoners since they were children, with their legs and necks fastened so that they can only look straight ahead of them and cannot turn their heads. What they can 'see' and what come into their view are shadows thrown by a fire onto the wall of the cave opposite them. Because of this, they believe the shadows are real objects and do not know that they merely reflected semblance of objects[6] . In both cases, there is a figure of a truth seeker, who after his journey of 'enlightenment', fails to convince his companions of what he has experienced. He remains a lonely figure as his new knowledge is never grasped by his companions. But there are striking differences between Plato's cave and Cervantes' cave. In the former, the search for truth is allegorized as an upward movement towards light and truth is believed to be out of the cave. In the latter case, Don Quixote seeks truth in darkness in the cave, believing the truth is down in there. Hence, the journey of the search for truth is allegorized as a downward movement. Don Quixote's 'enlightenment' is down within the cave, not outside it.

It would be simplistic to view the descent into the Cave of Montesinos as a comical reverse of the ascent out of Plato's cave. In Plato's cave, the site of illusion is within the cave, but in the Cave of Montesinos, bewitchment is found both inside and outside the cave. On one level, both Plato's cave and Cervantes' cave are places of tropelía and through illusion and bewitchment, no subjectivity can

---

Charles Jarvis (Oxford edition, 1992, p. 965) thinks likewise, but Tobias Smollett regards this as a mistake in the original (2001 Modern Library Paperback Edition, p. 1116). Edith Grossman, however, does not comment on this in her translation.

6 T.Z. Lavine in *From Socrates to Sartre: the Philosophic Quest* (New York: Bantam Books, 1984) suggests Plato's Cave could be regarded as a critique of everyday lives and science, a political allegory, an allegory of the philosopher-king and an allegory of despair and hope (pp. 28–30); while Frederick Copleston in *A History of Philosophy Vol. 1: Greece and Rome* (New York: Image Books, 1993) believes Plato's cave allegorizes an epistemological progress (pp. 160–62).

be stabilized. What one encounters are only shadows and reflections. On another level, the significance of the underground cave-dwelling in Plato's allegory lies in its contrast to the truth outside itself, but such a contrast is absent from the Cave of Montesinos. What Don Quixote experiences within the cave mirrors the one outside it. Bewitchment and destabilization are found both inside and outside the cave. Whether the cave represents Don Quixote's dream reality or not, his cave adventure reveals that it is impossible to escape such destabilizing bewitchment and hence Don Quixote has to embark on a utopian pursuit through the imaginary reality of chivalry to reconcile the paradoxes and contradictions he experiences. Furthermore, this also means that the cave as a space of tropelía mirrors the outer world as an even bigger space of bewitchment, drowning everybody with tropelía.

In the Cave of Montesinos, tropelía turns Don Quixote's reality into a dream which is simultaneously liberating and repressive. His adventure in the cave is both anachronistic and utopian. The tropelía he experiences is a space of perpetual displacement. His adventure reveals that Don Quixote is in favour of bewitchment. If this is Don Quixote's wish, his dream in the cave fulfills his wish and so, Dulcinea will never be disenchanted inside the cave, because the moment of Dulcinea's disenchantment may mean the closure of the narrative. The cave also represents Don Quixote's heroism of imagination, which is manifested through tropelía. Through tropelía, he is able to deal with fiction, to turn lies into truth, especially Sancho's lies of bewitchment. In this light, Don Quixote is a postmodern figure and the distinction between truth and falsehood no longer holds and is no longer necessary. Moreover, going down the cave, for Don Quixote, is a particular kind of tropelía. It is a tropelía in the form of 'enlightenment'. The cave has such a bewitching power of tropelía, because of which the reader is enchanted and drawn into it. To both the reader and Don Quixote, this tropelía is already enlightenment and because of which Don Quixote is 'enlightened'. What Don Quixote shows through his adventure in the cave is enlightenment as bewitchment, or bewitchment as enlightenment. When we think we are enlightened, it is possible that actually we are bewitched. When we attempt to enlighten others, as in the project of colonialism, we are actually bewitching the others.

On another level, a narrative can also be regarded as the archive which is part of bewitchment. In these two texts of Cervantes, when the reader enters the narrative of Berganza's autobiography through Campunzo's manuscript and when the reader enters the Cave of Montesinos together with Don Quixote, he is already in the grip of the bewitching power of tropelía, which comes in the form of feminine seduction. This strange adventure in the Cave of Montesinos is of paramount importance to the whole *Don Quixote* in that after this adventure, Don Quixote's narrative cannot establish itself as Sancho Panza is no longer sure whether Don Quixote is telling the truth. This is the effect of tropelía by which truth and lies, reality and appearance are confused and destabilized. In other words, Sancho Panza is bewitched by Don Quixote's narrative. This is the power of tropelía the story-teller has in his / her storytelling which bewitches the listener / reader, like what Scheherazade does to sultan Schahriar in *The Arabian Nights* – bewitching him through the tropelía of story-telling in order to defer death. Death is the very opposite of tropelía as in death, identity is fixed while in tropelía, identity is always destabilized and transforming.

4.3. Second Nature and Knight-Errantry

Don Quixote's utopianism can best be unpacked through Nietzsche's postmodern concepts of the first nature and the second nature. Nietzsche in 'On the Uses and Disadvantages of History for Life' says that 'if he is to live, man must possess and from time to time employ the strength to break up and dissolve a part of the past' (Nietzsche 1997, 75). He explains the necessity for this break:

> For since we are the outcome of earlier generations, we are also the outcome of their aberrations, passions and errors, and indeed of their crimes; it is not possible wholly to free oneself from this chain. If we condemn these aberrations and regard ourselves as free of them, this does not alter the fact that we originate in them. (Nietzsche 1997, 76)

If one wants to free oneself from the chain of the past, it is to no avail if he only condemns what he inherits from earlier generations, including their aberrations, passions, errors and crimes. It is also not impossible to repress this fact by cheating himself into thinking that he is free of them. Nietzsche suggests that

> The best we can do is to confront our inherited and hereditary nature with our knowledge, and through a new, stern discipline combat our inborn heritage and inplant [sic] in ourselves a new habit, a new instinct, a second nature, so that our first nature withers away. It is an attempt to give oneself, as it were *a posteriori*, a past in which one would like to originate in opposition to that in which one did originate: - always a dangerous attempt because it is so hard to know the limit to denial of the past and because second natures are usually weaker than first. (Nietzsche 1997, 76) (original italics)

What one needs to do is a direct confrontation with his inherited and hereditary first nature, combat and raid it so as to forge a new habit, a second nature, a new origin which is 'posteriori'. This utopian future free of the chain of aberrations of the earlier generations can be achieved only through a will to construct a past, a new origin, a new beginning. It is only with the presence of this second nature that the first nature will wither away. Nietzsche knows how difficult it is to forge a new second nature, but he reminds us that 'there is even a noteworthy consolation: that of knowing that this first nature was once a second nature and that every victorious second nature will become a first' (Nietzsche 1997, 77). The past is no longer fixed or unalterable, but is malleable. What Don Quixote attempts to achieve is a utopian second nature free from the chain of aberrations of the first nature through tropelía, to raid and alter the past, to forge a new past and a second nature, in the hope that a utopia for the future can be created. As the first nature was once the second nature, this second nature forged out of tropelía will soon become the first.

In this way, one is no longer told what he is or he does not have to inherit the legacies of the earlier generations, but he can have his own origin and past, and hence his future.

It is through tropelía that Don Quixote creates his own reality manifested in the form of knight-errantry, which is from his library of books on chivalry and knight-errantry. It is due to the destruction of his stationary, static library as his archive that he embarks upon adventures one after the other. This destruction of his immobile archive only precipitates and crystallizes the beginning of his utopian attempt to disenchant Dulcinea and the world. It is through tropelía that his imagination, ideals and archive are not only kept alive, but also spread to others. It seems the death of one archive will only lead to the birth of another one, no matter whether it is of a different nature or of a different form.[7] Don Quixote's library archive is raided and destroyed, but through his knight-errantry, he successfully saves his own archive by creating a past that no longer exists, a past that has been turned into ashes. Don Quixote's knight-errantry, in this regard, is not only an activity of writing, but also an activity of raiding, through which it creates its history, its world and most importantly, it creates a past that the present denies. Now Don Quixote's present is justified by the past that he has created in his fluid, mobile landless archive, and through tropelía, he creates his own reality. The past is raided, re-written and re-created so as to allow a possibility of the future. Because of this, he dares to make adventures and misadventures for the future.

To Don Quixote, knight-errantry is an activity of writing and raiding, and through which on the one hand, he raids and unburdens himself from the legacies of the past, the first nature, and on the other, he rewrites his own past, his world and his second nature. He constructs his own world and believes that this world of his own creation is true. In this sense, Don Quixote creates his own life and the life he has created becomes his 'real' life. Ultimately, not only Don Quixote, but other people at the end of the story, especially Sancho Panza, believe the reality that Don Quixote has created without a past, or with a new past, with a past that no longer exists.

'The Dialogue of the Dogs' and Don Quixote's adventure in the Cave of Montesinos exemplify two kinds of tropelía, resulting in two kinds of utopianism. In the former text, the manuscript is presented in the form of intertextuality, with a beginning foretold in its preceding story 'The Deceitful Marriage'. This manuscript is a destabilizing narrative, depicting tropelía of a witch at the core of the text. In this text, tropelía is the magic of a witch speaking in allegorical language which reveals Berganza's past, explains his present state and predicts his future. Hence, Berganza's utopian dream is to reclaim his past by returning to his own human guise. In other words, he wishes to undo the magical transformation and the tropelía on him.

---

[7] Rapaport in *Later Derrida: Reading the Recent Work* talks about the 'landed archive' and the landless archive' on p. 79, for example. A 'landed archive' may refer to the one with concrete entity spatially immobile while a 'landless archive' may refer to memory, electronic data, etc., which are not confined by space.

Don Quixote's adventure in the Cave of Montesinos is presented as a strange interpolating episode in which tropelía unsettles reality both inside and outside the cave. It is never sure whether Don Quixote brings tropelía into the cave after he has internalized the trick that Sancho Panza plays on him in Part 2, Chapter 10, or whether he comes out of the cave with tropelía in his narrative for Sancho Panza. In both possibilities, Sancho Panza plays an important role. In the former case, he is the source of Don Quixote's tropelía within the cave, while in the latter, he inherits this tropelía and embarks on his process of Quixotification.

In the cave, tropelía destabilizes not only the reality that Don Quixote is experiencing, but also patriarchy of the homogenizing cave. The certainty of time, place and events is no longer guaranteed. This tropelía is cast not only on Don Quixote, but also on Dulcinea. Unlike the witch as the source of tropelía in Berganza's autobiography, Dulcinea is the victim here and hence, Don Quixote's task is to undo such bewitching tropelía. This utopianism of Don Quixote can also be read as his attempt to unburden his first nature, his 'inherited and hereditary' past by means of knight-errantry in order to create a second nature, a new past for a utopian future.

Cervantes leaves to the writers and raiders of the archive after him a 'lost' archive of tropelía, bewitchment, liberation and utopia. Don Quixote's library is burned feverishly to ashes by the priest and it is an archive damned by the others as the source of Don Quixote's madness (Part 1, Chapter 6, 50–52). The archive is gone, but Cervantes' spectre is still around, haunting the raiders and writers of the archive, like Borges, Puig and García Márquez.

PART 3
Post-colonial Archives

Chapter 5
Borges: Lost in the Library

> The Renaissance explores the universe; the baroque explores libraries.
>
> Benjamin[1]

> I … had always thought of Paradise
> In form and image as a library.
>
> Borges[2]

> - in archival documents: these are my childhood memories, just as impenetrable as are such documents when I do not know their provenance
>
> Lacan[3]

> Flaubert is to the library what Manet is to the museum. They both produced works in a self-conscious relationship to earlier paintings or texts – or rather to the aspect in painting or writing that remains indefinitely open.
>
> Foucault[4]

Borges, Puig and García Márquez write in the shadow of Cervantes and inherit his memories, and their raiding of the archive can be regarded as Latin America's response to Spain's colonization. Borges is in fear of being marginalized by colonial Spain and thus, emphasizes the versatility of Argentine writers who can write beyond their culture and tradition[5]. Puig's *Kiss of the Spider Woman* was written in 1976, in a period of Isabella Perón's despotic rule of Argentine (1974–76) after the death of her husband Juan Domingo Perón in 1974.[6] In addition to this critique

---

1 Walter Benjamin, *The Origin of German Tragic Drama* trans. John Osborne (London and New York: Verso, 1998), p. 140 (first published as *Ursprung des deutschen Trauerspiels* in 1963).

2 Jorge Luis, Borges, 'Poem of the Gifts' in *Selected Poems* (Harmondsworth, Penguin Books, 2000), p. 95.

3 Jacques Lacan, *Écrits: A Selection* trans. Alan Sheridan (New York and London: W.W. Norton and Co., 1977), p. 50.

4 Michel Foucault, *Language, Counter-memory, Practice: Selected Essays and Interviews* trans. Donald F. Bouchard and Sherry Simon (Ithaca, New York: Cornell University Press, 1977), p. 92.

5 See Borges's *The Total Library: Non-Fiction 1922–1986* trans. Esther Allen, Suzanne Jill Levine and Eliot Weinberger (Harmondsworth: Penguin Books, 1999), p. 423. This will be discussed at a later stage in this chapter.

6 See *History of Argentina* by Daniel K. Lewis (Westport: Greenwood Press, 2001), pp. 140–44.

of Isabella Perón's fascist regime, the novel can also be read as a reaction against Argentina's supposed Spanish-Christian heritage which was stressed by the military governments during 1976 to 1983 under the doctrine of national security (Rock 1993, 228–31). This sentiment is implicit in the novel not only through Molina as a figure of anti-authority, but also through recasting Don Quixote's knight-errantry as seductive narration and his chivalry as sexual de-orientation. García Márquez's *Chronicle of a Death Foretold*, in this light, can also be seen as writing in line with Cervantes, but playfully re-dressing him as an anti-religious brothel owner in a Catholic town visited by a bishop who refuses to come ashore to bless the people. These three raiders and writers of the archive paradoxically remain in Cervantes' shadow, writing with the spectre of Cervantes behind them, and at the same time are playful with Cervantes' shadow. Their raiding is executed through their writing and in their postcolonial response, writing is raiding, and the writer is the raider.

While for Cervantes, tropelía is a means to transform the paralyzing reality and homogenizing 'first nature' into a 'second nature' of a new past, Borges, writing in the shadow of Cervantes, warns the reader of the danger of such a paralyzing domination of the archive in the form of memory and describes a utopian library of Babel in which the feverish archive is all-encompassing but non-homogenizing. This chapter focuses on two of his short stories, 'Funes the Memorious'[7] and 'The Library of Babel'.[8] The former can be regarded as Borges's response to Cervantes' 'The Glass Graduate', while the latter is answered by Eco's *The Name of the Rose*,[9] in which there is a diabolical librarian named Jorge of Burgos, who not only eats up poisoned manuscripts, but also burns the library into ashes.

5.1. Funes and Paralyzing Memory

In 'The Glass Graduate', one of Cervantes' *Exemplary Stories*, Tomás Rodaja, alias the Glass Graduate, is a paradoxical character in that, on the one hand, he cannot even remember his parents, their names and his own name and where he is from. This implies an impairment of his memory. On the other hand, he is gifted with 'a formidable memory':

> … in the eight years he remained with them [that is, his two masters who have looked after him since they found him asleep beneath a tree along the bank of the River Tormes] he became so famous in the university for his fine intellect and remarkable ability that he was esteemed and beloved by all kinds of people. His main subject of study was law, but the discipline in which he distinguished

---

7 'Funes the Memorious' in Jorge Luis Borges's *Labyrinths* trans. James E. Irby (Harmondsworth: Penguin Books, 1964), pp. 87–95. Another translation entitled 'Funes, His Memory' is by Andrew Hurley in *Collected Fictions, Jorge Luis Borges* (Harmondsworth: Penguin Books, 1998), pp. 131–7.

8 In *Labyrinths*, pp. 78–86, and in *Collected Fictions, Jorge Luis Borges*, pp. 112–18.

9 Umberto Eco, *The Name of the Rose*, trans. William Weaver (London: Minerva, 1992).

> himself best was the humanities. He possessed such a formidable memory and it was so enlightened by his good judgement and breadth of mind that he was no less famous for the one than for the other. (106–7)

The story unfolds with Tomás Rodaja as an 11-year-old boy in peasant clothing, with an impaired memory. Then he becomes a scholar with 'a formidable memory', specializing in law and preferring books to women. Soon he is lured into drinking a love potion in a Toledan quince by a Moorish woman, who attempts to seduce him through the power of the drink. But her plan goes awry and he becomes mad, thinking that he has changed from a man of flesh to a man of glass.

He is a person doubly repressed. The memory of his past is repressed right at the beginning, and although his memory shows a formidable power which helps him make good judgement and manifest breadth of mind in his scholastic pursuit which can be regarded as patriarchal machinery, his excellence in memory does not restore the memory that he has previously repressed. Worse still, this excellence in the patriarchal setting is shattered by feminine seduction in the form of a Toledan quince by which his flesh body is turned into glass from the inside. This agent who undoes his mental excellence is not simply a woman, but a foreign Moorish woman, a witch-like figure, like Rojas' Celestina and Cervantes' Cañizares in 'The Dialogue of the Dogs'. This foreign Moorish woman is in a position outside patriarchy in a double sense. Being a woman is already an outsider in a patriarchal structure and this outsideness is doubled by her foreign Moorish identity. In this regard, the implication of the presence of this mysterious Moorish woman is a double unsettling of patriarchy.

After the drink, the Glass Graduate embarks on his second stage of repression, but this time, it is the repression of his body. He symbolizes the workings of both internal (his memory) and external (his body) repression, a repression both from the inside (his own repression of his memory) and from the outside (his repression caused by the Moorish woman). This repressive character of Cervantes is echoed by Borges's Ireneo Funes in his story 'Funes the Memorious' (or 'Funes, His Memory'), an ordinary and rural boy in a remote region of Uruguay, who can tell the time of day without resorting to a watch. This 'chronometrical' Funes can internalize external time (*Labyrinths*, 1964, 89). The issue of memory is made conspicuous by the narrator's repetitive phrase 'I remember …' in the opening paragraph:

> *I remember* him (I have no right to utter this sacred verb, only one man on earth had that right and he is dead) with a dark passion flower in his hand, seeing it as no one has ever seen it, though he might look at it from the twilight of dawn till that of evening, a whole lifetime. *I remember* him, with his face taciturn and Indian-like and singularly remote, behind the cigarette. *I remember* (I think) his angular, leather-braiding hands. *I remember* near those hands a maté gourd bearing the Uruguayan coat of arms; *I remember* a yellow screen with a vague lake landscape in the window of his house. *I clearly remember* his voice: the slow, resentful, nasal voice of the old-time dweller of the suburbs, without the Italian sibilants we have today. (87) (italics added)

The six repetitive phrases of 'I remember …' indicate that the narrator has inherited Funes' memory. They flow from the whole to the part, from the concrete to the abstract – the narrator's memory of Funes moves from his whole person with a dark passion flower in his hand, then to his taciturn, Indian-like face, then to his angular hands, then to the maté gourd near his hands, then to the yellow screen in the window of his house, and finally, to his abstract voice, which is a slow, resentful, nasal one of the dweller of the suburbs. In addition, this story is about Funes, who changes from an ordinary rural boy to a person with the gift of absolute memory after his being thrown down from a horse. But in terms of narrative time, before he gains this extraordinary gift of remembering, he is first remembered by the narrator. Before the whole world becomes his object of observation and memory under his subjection, he is the object of the narrator's memory and the subject of his narration. By the repetitive phrase 'I remember (him)', a difference is made, a distance created, a relationship established between the narrator and Funes – the narrator being an Argentine, Funes a Uruguayan; the rememberer and the remembered; the ordinary and the extraordinary; the mobile and the immobile; the narrator and the narratee. Before the narrator shifts to Funes' extraordinary gift of absolute memory, he first stresses how Funes is remembered, by moving from the memories of Funes' concrete bodily features to his abstract voice, from the memory of the concrete to the one of the abstract.

The influence of Cervantes on Borges can be traced through the similarities between the Glass Graduate and Ireneo Funes. Both of them are gifted with memory, the former with a 'formidable memory' while the latter with an 'absolute' one. The Glass Graduate, after drinking the Toledan quince and after his body is repressed to glass, is like a relic housed in a glass receptacle that nobody is allowed to come close to, while Funes, before his memory changes from the ordinary to the extraordinary, is known for 'certain peculiarities such as avoiding contact with people' (88). The identities of the Glass Graduate's parents remain a mystery, while in Funes' case, although it is known that he is the son of the ironing woman in town, called María Clementina Funes, people's views on the identity of his father are divided: 'some people said his father was a doctor at the meat packers, an Englishman by the name of O'Connor, and others that he was a horse tamer or scout from the Salto district' (88).

Despite all these similarities between the Glass Graduate and Funes, the issue of repression is manifested in different forms. The repression that the Glass Graduate effects is of both his memory and his body, which in turn, represses the other – the memory of the other and the physical contact with the other, while the repression of Funes' body comes in the form of paralysis, a deprival of physical, bodily mobility, which comes with his gift of absolute memory after his fall from a half-tamed horse. The gift of his extraordinary, absolute memory comes at the expense of his physical mobility, of the deprival of his bodily movement. Because of this, he becomes 'a perpetual prisoner' (89), confined in a little dark room, which is his archive abounding not only in manuscripts or parchments, but also in memories. In this little dark room, his memory cannot stop working and his faculty of perception takes away his subjectivity. He cannot choose to stop remembering his world around him. Everything is new and fresh (93–4). The present to him is simply 'intolerable in its richness and sharpness, as were his most distant and trivial memories' (91). His memory is so total and absolute that not only the minute details of the object in his sight, but also their muscular and thermal sensations are remembered. His ability of absolute memory is not confined to the real world:

> He could reconstruct all his dreams, all his half-dreams. Two or three times he had reconstructed a whole day; he never hesitated, but each reconstruction had required a whole day. He told me: 'I alone have more memories than all mankind has probably had since the world has been the world.' And again: 'My dreams are like you people's waking hours.' And again, towards dawn: 'My memory, sir, is like a garbage heap.' (92)

It is ironic that his extraordinary memory is like 'a garbage heap' and this reveals the second type of repression that Funes is suffering from. Though he is gifted with this extraordinary power of memory, he is at the same time deprived of the ability to forget. Because of his inability to forget, to unremember, memories are like fragments and ruins piling up on top of each other. Borges's foregrounding of Funes' extra-ordinary memory faculty reveals his own fear of being dominated and marginalized. In 'The Argentine Writer and Tradition', he points out that while people believe Argentine history should be defined as a desire to move away from Spain and its influence, he says Argentine writers show their versatility through writing like the Spanish.[10] This is a post-colonial response to the European colonization and domination which claims that writing should be coloured with its local culture, which in Borges's view is a recent European cult. Argentine writing should not be confined by its own culture, like Shakespeare writing on Scandinavian subject matter in *Hamlet* and on a Scottish theme in *Macbeth.*

Funes not only fails to forget, but he also fails to make generalization and abstraction. To him, the dog seen at 3:14 and then at 3:15 can never be the same dog, and hence it is 'difficult for him to comprehend that the generic symbol *dog* embraces so many unlike individuals of diverse size and form' (93, original italics). The narrator at the beginning of the story 'remembers' Funes from the concrete images to the abstract, but at the end of the story, Funes is always in the world of the present, bombarded by the incessant influx of images from the external world through his faculty of perception. In this sense, he is only a receptacle of images, a passive receiver of images from the external world, a slave of perception who has lost his subjectivity and his ability to choose, to forget and to generalize. As a result, he can remember but cannot think, as the narrator says:

> With no effort, he had learned English, French, Portuguese and Latin. I suspect, however, that he was not very capable of thought. To think is to forget differences, generalize, make abstractions. In the teeming world of Funes, there were only details, almost immediate in their presence. (94)

---

[10] In Borges's *The Total Library: Non-Fiction 1922–1986*, p. 423.

Though he can remember things down to the minute spatial and temporal details, his memories of these things are simply useless, like a 'garbage heap'. What is being repressed besides his physical mobility is his ability to forget, to generalize, to make abstraction, and above all, to think. Funes, in this light, is actually like a computer that only records and stores data, but can never make a generalization out of them. His gift of memory takes away not only his subjectivity, but also his humanness by turning him into an entity with a memory like a machine. The ultimate repression that Funes suffers is the repression of his status of being a human and of his subjectivity. If so, when the narrator says 'I remember him' at the beginning of his narrative, what he wants to draw the reader's attention to may be the difference between human and machine.

In fact, his name Ireneo Funes is oxymoronic. His surname 'Funes' is strongly suggestive of the meanings 'funereal', 'ill-fated' and 'dark',[11] while his first name 'Ireneo' is the masculine form of 'Irene', who is a Greek goddess of peace (the Greek word *eirēnē* means 'peace') (*OED*). So, 'Ireneo Funes' means a funereal, ill-fated, dark peace, the peace of funeral, the peace of death, a peaceful death and the death of peace. Funes dies in his little dark room, which is his archive full of inevitable and indelible memories. Memory is his archive and he gets lost in this archive of memory because his faculty of perception incessantly accumulates images. He dies of lung congestion, paralleling his mental congestion.

The evil of Funes' memory as archive is that it is paralyzing in nature. Funes is incapable of escaping from his archive of memory, because memory, in a metaphorical sense, paralyzes his mobility, his ability to forget, his power of generalization of abstraction and finally his thinking. This shows the paralyzing power of memory and the consequence is a deprival and denial of subjectivity in this archive of memory.

The similarities and differences between Funes and the Glass Graduate reveal how Borges writes in the shadow of Cervantes, replying to him by reversing the Glass Graduate. First, while the Glass Graduate is lacking in memory and having a glass body which paralyzes his connection to the other, Funes is paralyzed in terms of not only his physical immobility, but also the deprival of his subjectivity and thinking. Not only is he drowned in his lungs, he is also overwhelmed by his archive of memory. This is because of his excessive memories, his indiscriminate accumulation of memories and his inability to save himself by generalization and logical thinking. Funes gets lost in his own archive, loses his bearings in the labyrinth of his memories and misses his tread for getting out this labyrinth of paralysis. In this sense, he is a masculine archon emasculated by and imprisoned in his own archive. Second, both the Glass Graduate and Funes are de-humanized – the human quality of the former is reduced to a body of glass while that of the latter a faithful and loyal body functioning like a machine which records every detail of the images seen without imposing any judgement, alternation or generalization.

[11] This implication is from *Borges and His Fiction: A Guide to His Mind and Art* by Gene H. Bell-Villada (Austin: University of Texas Press, 1999), p. 106.

But this similarity between them is also their difference. The difference between the Glass Graduate and Funes becomes the one between unconscious forgetting and inevitable remembering, between glass and machine, between a light, fragile entity symbolizing paranoia, irrational distrust and fear of the other, and a heavy, mighty contrivance symbolizing an irrational, indiscriminate and incessant intake of the other, and between fragility and ephemerality on the one hand, and solidity and permanence on the other. Cervantes' Glass Graduate, who is lacking in memory, is now turned into Borges's Ireneo Funes, who has a mighty ability of memory, which is a useless garbage heap, a peaceful funeral of subjectivity and an archive of death.

This immobile and dehumanized hero of Borges's is from Uruguay, a country between Argentina and Brazil. The narrator remembers his hands and a maté gourd in this way:

> I remember near those hands a maté gourd bearing the Uruguayan coat of arms … (*Labyrinths*, trans. by James E. Irby, 1964, 87)
>
> I recall near those hands a *mate* cup, with the coat of arms of the Banda Oriental. (*Collected Fictions, Jorge Luis Borges*, trans. by Andrew Hurley, 1998, 131) (original italics)

The Banda Oriental, the 'eastern bank' of the River Plate, is the old name of Uruguay before it became a country. Funes is remembered by and reduced into a pair of hands with a maté gourd which bears the coat of arms of Uruguay, the old memory of his homeland before its birth. There is a connection between Funes and the history of Uruguay, which is untold and hidden by the narrator. Uruguay, before the arrival of Europeans, was a territory supporting groups of semi-nomadic people, no more than 5,000 to 10,000 in population. The first European to explore and raid Uruguay was the Spanish navigator Juan Diaz de Solis in 1516, followed by Portuguese navigator Ferdinand Magellan in 1520. Since 1620s, Jesuit and Franciscan missions had been established and hence, the indigenous population had begun to collapse and to be raided. The Spanish raiding and colonization begun in 1624, followed by Portuguese settlement in 1680. The Spanish rule was revolted against only in 1820.

When the constitution for the Oriental State of Uruguay was approved on July 18, 1830, the country had scarcely 74,000 inhabitants. However, Uruguay's first years of independence were perilous and disastrous. Not only had 20 years of war greatly reduced cattle numbers, the lands and fortunes of many colonial families had been destroyed. This newly established country at the same time was greatly troubled by its internal conflicts. The factions of the first and second presidents, José Frutuoso Rivera and Manuel Oribe, battled each other in what was known as the Guerra Grande (Great War). Oribe and his followers, called the Blanco (White) party, controlled the interior, while Rivera and his adherents used red colours and became the Colorado (Red) Party, based in Montevideo. In 1851, the Guerra Grande ended without a clear victory for either side – the Uruguayan interior was devastated, the government bankrupt.

These internal conflicts opened up chances for intervention by foreign powers. In 1865, the Colorados were able to oust the Blancos from power only with the aid of a Brazilian army. Uruguay, together with Brazil and Argentina involved in the War of the Triple Alliance (1864–70) in order to combat the threats of Paraguay. Though Paraguay was defeated, Uruguay's commerce was disrupted by persistent political disputes – a civil war known as the Revolution of the Lances (1868–72), and Brazilian and Argentine involvement in Uruguayan affairs. In 1876, the Uruguayan armed forces took over the government and began to establish firmer control over the interior. However, public support for the government eventually died down because of the brutal and corrupt leaderships, and a civilian Colorado government returned to power in 1890.[12] Funes (first seen by the narrator in 1884, died in 1889) was situated in such a period of Uruguayan history full of internal and external conflicts.

Young Funes, who dies when he is only 19 years old, symbolizes this newly established Uruguay. The development of this young country is retarded, warped and raided by both internal conflicts and external threats. It is paralyzed like Funes, who inevitably becomes a 'solitary and lucid spectator of a multiform, instantaneous and almost intolerably precise world' (*Labyrinths*, 1964, 94), difficult to sleep, incapable of thinking and generalization. Unlike Don Quixote and the Glass Graduate, who opt for arms and knight-errantry in order to create their archive, reality and future, Ireneo Funes does not and cannot take up arms because of his paralysis, nor does he write because his memory is already so precise and indelible that writing is not necessary. The archive he creates is made of memory piling upon each other like garbage. Here, this indicates that there are two kinds of archives – the archive forged out of utopian knight-errantry and the other out of indelible memory ready for recall.

Although Funes' memory is like a useless garbage heap, it is at the same time like writing because of its iterability. It may seem that his accumulation of memory like garbage 'piling upon each other' is at odds with the idea of iterability, but they are not necessarily contradictory as the former points to the fact that such accumulation of memory excludes the possibility of generalization and abstraction, thus depriving Funes of 'thinking', while the latter refers to his ability to recall his memory, to iterate the image in his head to the minute details.

Derrida in *Limited Inc* points out that, iterability as a marker of writing entails both 'repetition' and 'alterity' (or difference) in that the Latin root 'iter' of the word 'iterate' means 'again', but in the Sanskrit, 'itara' means 'other' (Derrida 1988, 7 and 62). Whenever a sentence or a mark is reused in a different context, it does not remain the same. In this regard, first of all, iterability ties repetition to alterity. Second, iterability is a force of rupture by which an utterance or a mark can break with its original context. However, this rupture of meaning exists even if a sentence or an utterance appears only once and never appears again, never to

[12] "Uruguay" *Encyclopaedia Britannica* from Encyclopaedia Britannica Online. http://search.eb.com/eb/article?eu=115675.

be iterated or altered by being inserted in a new context. It is already, from the beginning, divided within itself. It is splitting in nature because of its iterability and such a mark or sentence is already divided. Iterability is différance, that is, an opening within the utterance itself that makes it differ from itself, within itself. At the same time, the utterance or the mark can be cut off from the intention of the original mark or utterance. The originator may be absent or dead, but the mark still functions, just as it goes on functioning after the death of its intended recipient.

Derrida illustrates this absence of the originator by a 'shopping list'. The moment I make my shopping list, I know that it implies my absence, that it already detaches itself from me in order to function beyond my 'present' act and that it is utilizable at another time. The sender of the shopping list is not the same as the receiver, even if they bear the same name and the identity (Derrida 1988, 49). When I walk into the supermarket, I do not have to be shopping on behalf of another person in order to be different. When looking at my list, I (the receiver) am not the same as the sender. So, a shopping list implies not only the splitting, the differing and deferring of presence and identity, not only a force of rupture from its original context, but also the absence of the sender and the receiver. Because of iterability, the list is still readable to the others, even after the death of the sender or the receiver.[13]

Funes' memory behaves likewise. His ability to make his memory iterable, retrievable whenever needed. If so, his formidable memory signifies his absence and death. But the iterability of his memory is different from what Derrida describes in the sense that his memory cannot be iterable and iterated by the others, as the others do not have this faculty of Funes' to preserve and retrieve memory to such a precise extent. It dies and vanishes with his death. This iterability of memory, which is also the cause of his ruinous memory and his death, exists only in Funes, like the iterability of data only in specific types of computer systems, not in the other incompatible ones.

It is ironic that what raids and destroys his archive, ruins the ruinous heap of his memory and finally leads to his drowning in his lungs and memories is his own extraordinary faculty for preserving memories. Funes has created an archive of memory too excessive for him, a present made up of indiscriminate accumulation of facts, and a reality he cannot bear. Funes symbolizes a period of time in which the country is threatened by internal battles and external menaces. He reveals the dangers of the archive in the form of memory indelible and iterable as writing. He is also a warning about the apprehensive future in which mechanical recording of facts in the manner of indiscriminate accumulation will turn the world into a garbage heap of useless memory and data.

---

[13] In 'Signature Event Context.' in *Limited Inc* trans. Samuel Weber and Jeffrey Mehlman, pp. 7–8; also in *Margins of Philosophy*, trans. Alan Bass (Chicago: The University of Chicago Press, 1982), pp. 315–16.

5.2. Borges's Library

Funes' little dark room is his archive which houses not manuscripts or parchments, but memories. His memories, which are absolute and total, are his manuscripts. His archive is his library, as total and chaotic as the total library described in Borges's another short story 'The Library of Babel'. This library, which can also be regarded as the universe, is composed of 'an indefinite and perhaps infinite number of hexagonal galleries' (*Labyrinths*, 1964, 78). The library is designed with identical cells:

> The distribution of the galleries is invariable. Twenty shelves, five long shelves per side, cover all the sides except two; their height, which is the distance from floor to ceiling, scarcely exceeds that of a normal bookcase. (78)

> There are five shelves for each of the hexagon's walls: each shelf contains thirty-five books of uniform format; each book is of four hundred and ten pages; each page, of forty lines, each line, of some eighty letters which are black in colour. (79)

Twenty-five orthographical symbols, which include the space, the comma, the period and the 22 letters of alphabet, are considered sufficient. Out of these symbols and out of the uniform design of the library, no two books are identical:

> *In the vast Library there are no two identical books*. … the Library is total and … its shelves register all the possible combinations of the twenty-odd orthographical symbols … all that it is given to express, in all languages. Everything: the minutely detailed history of the future, the archangels' autographies, the faithful catalogue of the Library, thousands and thousands of false catalogues, the demonstration of the fallacy of those catalogues, the demonstration of the fallacy of the true catalogue, the Gnostic gospel of Basilides, the commentary on that gospel, the commentary on the commentary on that gospel, the true story of your death, the translation of every book in all languages, the interpolations of every book in all books. (81–2) (original italics)

This total archive is raided and stretched by Borges and now it becomes all-encompassing, and through all the possible combinations of the 25 symbols, its books express everything. The library contains everything in the universe simply because it itself is the universe.[14] Likewise, Funes' little dark archive is this total

---

[14] For Borges's universe as a monstrous library, see 'The Great Library of Alexandria Burnt: Towards the History of a Symbol' by Jon Thiem, in *Journal of the History of Ideas*, Vol. 40, No. 4 (October–December 1979), pp. 507–26 (Baltimore: The Johns Hopkins University Press), especially p. 524; and 'Drawing Borges: A Two-Part Invention on the Labyrinths of Jorge Luis Borges and M.C. Escher' by Allene M. Parker, in *Rocky Mountain Review of Language and Literature*, Vol. 55, No. 2 (2001), pp. 11–23 (Salt Lake City: Rocky Mountain Modern Language Association). For Borges's obsession with total vision, see another article by Jon Thiem, 'Borges, Dantes and the Poetics of Total Vision' in

library in that, whatever comes into his perception is registered faithfully and totally down to the minute details. It is not mentioned that Funes has written anything, especially after his fall and after his acquiring his extraordinary memory faculty. In this respect, he is like Socrates and Confucius, both of whom did not set down their teaching and thoughts in black and white. Confucius' *Analects* was compiled by his disciples only after his death. Likewise, Socrates' dialogues were written by Plato. In fact, Funes' memory is so accurate that he does not need to turn his memories into writing. Another reason is that he simply cannot forget and if so, it is hardly necessary to record things in the form of writing. Third, it is not really possible for him to write out his thinking because his memories are so multitudinous and incessantly accumulative and because he cannot really think and generalize ideas.

Although books are written in an invariably orderly pattern in this total library of Babel, they are impenetrable. The 25 orthographical symbols were designed 300 years ago in view of solving the problem of 'the formless and chaotic nature of almost all the books':

> This much is already known: for every sensible line of straightforward statement, there are leagues of senseless cacophonies, verbal jumbles and incoherence. (I know of an uncouth region whose librarians repudiate the vain and superstitious custom of finding a meaning in books and equate it with that of finding a meaning in dreams or in the chaotic lines of one's palm.... They admit that the inventors of this writing imitated the twenty-five natural symbols, but maintain that this application is accidental and that the books signify nothing in themselves. This dictum, we shall see, is not entirely fallacious.) (80) (original ellipsis and bracketing)

What are embedded in an apparently straightforward, sensible and understandable statement are 'leagues of senseless cacophonies, verbal jumbles and incoherence'. To find a meaning in a book is as difficult as to find 'a meaning in dreams or in the chaotic lines of one's palm'. This impenetrable library can be described metaphorically by Borges's poem 'The Guardian of the Books':

> In my eyes there are no days. The shelves
> Are too high and my years do not reach them.
> Leagues of desert and dream besiege the tower.
> Why deceive myself?
> The truth is I've never known how to read,
> But I comfort myself thinking
> That the imagined and the past are one and the same (in *Selected Poems*, 2000, 283)

Comparative Literature, Vol. 40, No. 2 (Spring 1988), pp. 97–121 (Eugene: University of Oregon). For Borges's library as a means to expand our perception of fictional possibilities, see 'The Borders of Fiction' by Thomas Pavel, in *Poetics Today*, Vol. 4, No. 1 (1983), pp. 83–8 (Durham, NC: Duke University), and 'The Tales of Borges: Language and the Private Eye' by John Caviglia, in *MLN*, Vol. 89, No. 2, Hispanic Issue (March 1974), pp. 219–31 (Baltimore: The Johns Hopkins University Press).

The library's 'senseless cacophonies, verbal jumbles and incoherences' make itself impenetrable. What Borges foregrounds here is a poststructuralist issue, a philosophical concern–the dislocation of the signifier and the signified, and hence, the doubtful ability of writing to stabilize meaning. Underneath the signifier is something dream-like, fluid and chaotic. García Márquez follows this line to write a story without a plot, a signifier without a signified, which will be discussed in Chapter 7. This dislocation also implies that the link between the signifier and the signified should not be taken for granted and that meaning cannot be stabilized. The attempt to do so is like the search for a total book in the Library of Babel:

> On some shelf in some hexagon (men reasoned) there must exist a book which is the formula and perfect compendium of *all the rest*: some librarian has gone through it and he is analogous to a god. In the language of this zone vestiges of this remote functionary's cult still persist. Many wandered in search of Him. For a century they exhausted in vain the most varied areas. How could one locate the venerated and secret hexagon which housed Him? Someone proposed a regressive method. To locate book A, consult first a book B which indicates A's position; to locate book B, consult first a book C, and so on to infinity.... In adventures such as these, I have squandered and wasted my years. It does not seem unlikely to me that there is a total book on some shelf of the universe. (83–4) (original ellipsis and italics)

The narrator, like many others, has squandered and wasted many years, searching for this total book which is 'the formula and perfect compendium of all the rest', a book that is the formula and the original source of the existence of other books and at the same time, a perfect compendium to go along with them. Many inhabitants of the Library, including the narrator, are eager to get hold of this book because it can turn the reader who goes through it into a god, although it takes a painfully long period of time searching for it in a regressive manner. In order to get close to it and locate it, one has to get further away from it, which may lead to infinite regression. Though all these are known to the inhabitants of the Library and the pursuers of this total book, they are still persistent in their Quixotic quest. In the like manner, the author thinks he can stabilize meaning through writing and can express the meaning he wishes to convey because he still believes he is capable of mastering writing, and the reader when reading a text in front of him believes he comprehends the meaning of it because he still believes the meaning is anchored stably in the text.

This quest for the total book turns the inhabitants and librarians of the Library into Don Quixotes, and likewise, the quest for a meaning from a statement, or for a link between the signifier and the signified will turn the reader and the author alike into Don Quixotes too. The library, raided and rewritten by Borges, is a place where it is impossible to fix the link between the signifier and the signified. This results in destabilization of meaning and a chaotic Babel within the archive. Meanings can no longer be stabilized. This is a 'babelization' of the archive, and García Márquez writes in the same line and presents a babelization of voices in *Chronicle of a Death Foretold*. Despite such a babelization, and although the narrator of 'The Library of Babel' knows that he has already squandered and wasted many years, he, in the shadow of Don Quixote, still has a strong conviction that 'there is a total book on some shelf of the universe'. He in this sense is a Don Quixote whose birth and death are in this total archive, this unlimited library:

> Like all men of the Library, I have travelled in my youth; I have wandered in search of a book, perhaps the catalogue of catalogues; now that my eyes can hardly decipher what I write, I am preparing to die just a few leagues from the hexagon in which I was born. Once I am dead, there will be no lack of pious hands to throw me over the railing; my grave will be the fathomless air; my body will sink endlessly and decay and dissolve in the wind generated by the fall, which is infinite. (78–9)

He is a Don Quixote who has never left his library and whose knight-errantry is a search for this utopian total book. This archive is a place for both birth and death and its fathomless air is his grave. His dead body will sink and fall endlessly and infinitely, which even Lucifer may not anticipate.[15] 'The wind generated by the fall' will dissolve and decompose the body, which is far more destructive than the wind which disseminates Sibyl's scripted leaves. Still holding the belief of his Quixotic quest for the total book, the narrator speaks like praying:

> I pray to the unknown gods that a man – just one, even though it were thousands of years ago! – may have examined and read it. If honour and wisdom and happiness are not for me, let them be for others. Let heaven exist, though my place be in hell. Let me be outraged and annihilated, but for one instant, in one being, let Your enormous Library be justified. The impious maintain that nonsense is normal in the Library and that the reasonable (and even humble and pure coherence) is an almost miraculous exception. They speak (I know) of the 'feverish Library whose chance volumes are constantly in danger of changing into others and affirm, negate and confuse everything like a delirious divinity'. These words, which not only denounce the disorder but exemplify it as well, notoriously prove their authors' abominable taste and desperate ignorance. (84) (original bracketing)

The narrator speaks in a religious tone about the impious people's view that in this feverish Library, its volumes of books are in constant changes into others and behave like a 'delirious divinity' that affirm, negate and confuse everything. It is his belief that this delirious divinity manifest in the form of writing can turn everyone, including himself, into phantoms:

> The methodical task of writing distracts me from the present state of men. The certitude that everything has been written negates us or turns us into phantoms. I know of districts in which the young men prostrate themselves before books and kiss their pages in a barbarous manner, but they do not know how to decipher a single letter. (85)

---

[15] John Caviglia in 'The Tales of Borges: Language and the Private Eye' *MLN*, Vol. 89, No. 2, Hispanic Issue (March 1974), pp. 219–31 (Baltimore: The Johns Hopkins University Press) discusses the airshaft in the Library of Babel as an impossible fall and a void at the center of the story.

One of these men kissing their pages in a barbarous manner is taken up by Eco in *The Name of the Rose*. In this feverish library of Babel, what the librarians and inhabitants are searching for is not only the total book, but symbolically the origin of the universe. This desire to go back to the origin is like the desire for the primal scene which is the basis for their phantasies and which is always beyond their understanding.[16] But in Borges's library, the origin is not there, nor is the manuscript of such a total book. The knight-errantry of these Don Quixotes within this Library of Babel is also in vain. This is an archive in which whatever attempts to unpack it are ineffectual. In a post-colonial context, it is assumed that there is a colonial authority behind the archive, but when raiders and writers of the archive attempt to look for it, it is not there.

5.3. Eco's Library

This burning and feverish Library with books like a delirious divinity is echoed by the labyrinthine library in Umberto Eco's *The Name of the Rose*, which is guarded by a Spanish librarian, Jorge of Burgos. The setting of this novel is an isolated monastery. William of Baskerville and his scribe, Adso of Melk, arrive at the monastery in 1327 to initiate negotiations between Pope John XXII and a group of Franciscans who are critical of the Catholic Church's tolerant attitude towards wealth and its neglect of the poverty preached by Christ.[17] Their arrival coincides with a series of mysterious deaths, all connected with the monastery's library on the top floor of the Aedificium. Hence William begins to explore this labyrinthine library, in the hope of finding out the murderer.

The manuscript is central to the story, as the epigraph reads 'Naturally, a manuscript'. This stresses the importance of writing, here especially of handwriting and documents written (*scripti*) by hand (*manu*) as a relatively permanent medium for storing, retrieving and disseminating information. It is no coincidence that the story is set in 1327, about one century before the invention of the printing press (in the fifteenth century) and that's why what a library houses then were only manuscripts. In the novel, the manuscript that the monk scholars are pining for and debating

---

[16] For Freud's discussion on the primal scene, see his account of the case of the 'Wolf Man', in which Freud brings out different aspects of infantile neurosis: first, the act of coitus is understood by the child as father's aggression; second, the scene renders to the child both sexual excitation and castration anxiety; and third, the child interprets the scene as anal coitus. Also see *The Language of Psycho-Analysis* by J. Laplanche and J.-B. Pontalis, trans. Donald Nicholson-Smith (New York and London: W.W. Norton and Co., 1973), pp. 335–6.

[17] A detailed account of the tumultuous conflicts and changes in this period, like the conflicts between the Catholic Church and the Franciscans, the struggle for pre-eminence between the Pope and the Holy Roman Emperor, the decline in the Latin learning of the monasteries and the changes of social structures because of the accumulation of wealth in the cities, can be found in *A Distant Mirror: The Calamitous 14th Century* by Barbara Tuchman (Harmondsworth: Penguin, 1979).

is the second book of *Poetics* by Aristotle, which is an analysis of comedy and humour. In this light, the novel, right at the beginning (and beginnings since there is more than one beginning), foregrounds the importance of writing, of the manuscript and of the library. The novel centres on how the power of the manuscript causes violence and crimes. At the same time, the whole novel can be regarded as a non-originating manuscript. In this novel, there is not one, but three beginnings in three different narrative styles[18] – the first time in the style of a literary-historical discourse:

> On August 16, 1968, I was handed a book written by a certain Abbé Vallet, *Le Manuscrit de Dom Adson de Melk, traduit en français d'après l'édition de Dom J. Mabillon* (Aux Presses de l'Abbaye de la Source, Paris, 1842). Supplemented by historical information that was actually quite scant, the book claimed to reproduce faithfully a fourteenth-century manuscript that, in its turn, had been found in the monastery of Melk by the great eighteenth-century man of learning, … (1) (original italics and bracketing)

the second time in a theologico-philosophical tone in the Prologue to the main text:

> In the beginning was the Word and the Word was with God, and the Word was God. This was beginning with God and the duty of every faithful monk would be to repeat every day with chanting humility the one never-changing event whose incontrovertible truth can be asserted. But we see now through a glass darkly, and the truth, before it is revealed to all, face to face, we see in fragments (alas, how illegible) in the error of the world, so we must spell out its faithful signals even when they seem obscure to us and as if amalgamated with a will wholly bent on evil. (11) (original bracketing)

and the third time in a popular-cultural register of discourse[19]:

> It was a beautiful morning at the end of November. During the night it had snowed, but only a little, and the earth was covered with a cool blanket no more than three fingers high. In the darkness, immediately after lauds, we heard Mass in a village in the valley. Then we set off toward the mountain, as the sun first appeared. (21)

---

[18] See 'Gaudy Rose: Eco and Narcissism.' by Teresa de Lauretis, in *Reading Eco: An Anthology* ed. Rocco Capozzi (Bloomington and Indianapolis: Indiana University Press, 1997), Chapter 3.1, pp. 242–3. Her focus is on intertextuality and hybridity of this novel as a postmodern text, while my concern is on the non-originating characteristic of the manuscript.

[19] Eco makes his use of the popular-cultural register explicit in the following way:

'Is it possible to say "It was a beautiful morning at the end of November" without feeling like Snoopy? But what if I had Snoopy say it? If, that is, "It was a beautiful morning …" were said by someone capable of saying it, because in his day it was still possible, still not shopworn? A mask: that was what I needed.' in his *Postscript to The Name of the Rose*, trans. William Weaver (San Diego: Harcourt Brace Jovanovich Inc, 1984), p. 19.

The focus on writing and the manuscript is conspicuous given that among these three beginnings, two are concerned with writing and the manuscript. In the novel, this focus is placed on Aristotle's manuscript. It is ironic that on the one hand, this manuscript is on the analysis of comedy and humour, but on the other, the effects of this manuscript are the ones of desire, tragedy, violence and death. Since the whole plot whirls around this manuscript, William and Adso's task is to approach and decipher not only this manuscript, but also the connections among this manuscript, the library and the crimes and deaths in the monastery.

Before the two protagonists enter this gigantic and mysterious library, the story is unfolded as a 'whodunit' detective novel written in the style of Sherlock Holmes' adventures, in which William, like Sherlock Holmes, makes confident deductions to arrive at accurate facts.[20] His deductive brilliance is shown when he, without seeing or knowing Abbot Abo's favourite horse, can give its exact details and its whereabouts:

> "Come, come," William said, "it is obvious you are hunting for Brunellus, the abbot's favourite horse, fifteen hands, the fastest in your stables, with a dark coat, a full tail, small round hoofs, but a very steady gait; small head, sharp ears, big eyes. He went to the right, as I said, but you should hurry, in any case." (23)

and he teaches Adso the importance of observation of and attention to minute details given in symbols around the world:

> 'My good Adso," my master said, "during our whole journey I have been teaching you to recognize the evidence through which the world speaks to us like a great book. Alanus de Insulis said that
>
> *omnis mundi creatura*
> *quasi liber et pictura*
> nobis est in speculum[21]

[20] Detailed comparisons between *The Name of the Rose* and Sherlock Holmes' adventures can be found in Peter Bondanella's *Umberto Eco and the open text: Semiotics, fiction, popular culture*, Chapter 5 (Cambridge: Cambridge University Press, 1997); *Reading Eco: An Anthology*, ed. Rocco Capozzi, Chapters 3.1 and 3.2 (Bloomington and Indianapolis: Indiana University Press, 1997); 'Umberto Eco: *The Name of the Rose*' by Judy Ann Ford, in *The Detective as Historian: History and Art in Historical Crime Fiction*, ed. Ray B. Browne and Lawrence A. Kreiser, Jr., pp. 95–110 (Bowling Green, OH: Bowling Green State University Popular Press, 2000); and *Readers and Labyrinths: Detective Fiction in Borges, Bustos Domecq and Eco* by Jorge Hernández Martín (New York and London: Garland Publishing, Inc., 1995).

[21] The Latin reads:

every creature of the world
like a picture and a book
appears to us as a mirror

from *The Key to "The Name of the Rose"* by Adele J. Haft, Jane G. White and Robert J. White (Ann Arbor: The University of Michigan Press, 1999), p. 100.

> and he was thinking of the endless array of symbols with which God, through His creatures, speaks to us of the eternal life. But the universe is even more talkative than Alanus thought, and it speaks not only of the ultimate things (which it does always in an obscure fashion) but also of closer things, and then it speaks quite clearly. (23–4)

While Alanus is thinking of symbols as signs of God, William is a materialist and an empiricist, who suggests reading the signs 'not of ultimate things' but of the 'real' world much closer to us. His feat of deduction is based on the hoofprints in the snow, its size inferred from the proportions of the hooves, the direction indicated by a broken blackberry bush on the right fork of the road on which some long black horsehair has been caught, etc. By reading the implication imprinted on things and symbols around him, he becomes a semiotic detective, attempting to unveil more of the world through these signs.

William believes that Jorge of Burgos, the blind librarian who comes from Spain is the mastermind behind the crimes and deaths. Jorge delivers a dramatic sermon (397–407) full of and based on references to the Apocalypse, which mislead William into thinking that the crimes occur in the pattern mentioned in the Book of Revelation (8:6–10:10): seven murders occurring in seven days predictable by the guideline of the revelations of the seven seals[22]:

> Hail for [the first dead monk] Adelmo, … Blood for Venantius, … water for Berengar … the third part of the sky for Severinus … And finally scorpions for Malachi. (469–70)

However, things go awry when William, together with Adso, gradually explores the mysterious, Piranesi-like library, which is full of twisting staircases, secret passages, booby traps, and above all, secretive and authoritative manuscripts. Williams finds out that the monks' deaths, which seem to be in the Apocalyptic sequence, are actually 'random acts'. The crimes are not determined by an individual's scheme or by a single plot. There is no key to the chain of murders or any single plan for the murders. This reveals Borges's shadow on Eco, as this theme follows the one in Borges's 'Death and the Compass'. Instead, there is only a multiplicity of causes whose connections are discovered only by chance or mistake:

> "There was no plot," William said, "and I discovered it by mistake. … I have never doubted the truth of signs, Adso; they are the only things man has with which to orient himself in the world. What I did not understand was the relation

---

For more discussion on the symbols of book, see Ernst Robert Curtius' *Europe Literature and the Latin Middle Ages*, trans. Willard R. Trask (Princeton, NJ: Princeton University Press, 1983), Chapter 16, 'The Book as Symbol'.

[22] A detailed discussion of the pattern of the deaths in the monastery can be found in Peter Bondanella's *Umberto Eco and the open text: Semiotics, fiction, popular culture* (Cambridge: Cambridge University Press, 1997), Chapter 5, pp. 113–16.

> among signs. I arrived at Jorge through an apocalyptic pattern that seemed to underlie all the crimes, and yet it was accidental. I arrived at Jorge seeking one criminal for all the crimes and we discovered that each crime was committed by a different person, or by no one. I arrived at Jorge pursuing the plan of a perverse and rational mind, and there was no plan, or, rather, Jorge himself was overcome by his own initial design and there began a sequence of causes, and concauses, and of causes contradicting one another, which proceeded on their own, creating relations that did not stem from any plan. Where is all my wisdom, then? I behaved stubbornly, pursuing a semblance of order, when I should have known well that there is no order in the universe." (491–2)

William is no longer Sherlock Holmes and his deductive power fails him because causality becomes problematic and cannot be established. A sequence of causes, 'concauses' and self-contradicting causes proceed on their own and create relations and connections which do not stem from any plan. It seems William falls into a space of indescribable connections of events without centre or periphery, without causality or linearity. This space is a labyrinth without centre. Eco describes three types of labyrinth in his *Postscript to The Name of the Rose*. The first type is a classical Greek labyrinth, the labyrinth of Theseus:

> This kind does not allow anyone to get lost: you go in, arrive at the center, and then from the center you reach the exit. This is why in the center there is the Minotaur; if he were not there the story would have no zest, it would be a mere stroll. Terror is born, if it is born, from the fact that you do not know where you will arrive or what the Minotaur will do. But if you unravel the classical labyrinth, you find a thread in your hand, the thread of Ariadne. The classical labyrinth is the Ariadne's-thread of itself. (Eco 1984, 57)

If the archive of the monastery is a classical labyrinth, Jorge of Burgos the blind librarian and library guardian is the Minotaur. While the Minotaur in the Cretan labyrinth consumes human sacrifices, this blind minotaur in this medieval and evil library not only brings death to the other, but also eats up Aristotle's manuscript he has poisoned, which results in his being consumed by the very manuscript he consumes, by the library and by fire and ashes. There is no exit in the centre of the labyrinth, except death and ashes.

The second type is a mannerist labyrinth in which there are a lot of dead ends but there is only one exit:

> … if you unravel it, you find in your hands a kind of tree, a structure with roots, with many blind alleys. There is only one exit, but you can get it wrong. You need an Ariadne's thread to keep from getting lost. This labyrinth is a model of the trial-and-error process. (Eco 1984, 57)

If the library of the monastery is a mannerist labyrinth, William and Adso will get lost forever since there is no Ariadne's thread to help them find the exit. Causality cannot be their thread, as William admits that he unravels the crimes and discovers the connections among events by sheer chance.

The third type of labyrinth is a rhizomatic one, an idea from Deleuze and Guattari:

> … there is the net, or, rather, what Deleuze and Guattari call "rhizome." The rhizome is so constructed that every path can be connected with every other one. It has no center, no periphery, no exit, because it is potentially infinite. The space of conjecture is a rhizome space. The labyrinth of my library is still a mannerist labyrinth, but the world in which William realizes he is living already has a rhizome structure: that is, it can be structured but is never structured definitively. (Eco 1984, 57–8)

Deleuze and Guattari in *A Thousand Plateaus: Capitalism and Schizophrenia* describe a rhizome as a structure having 'neither beginning nor end, but always a middle from which it grows and which it overspills' (Deleuze and Guattari 1987, 21). The library, as well as the archive, is site for heterogeneous manuscripts without necessary connections or links. This is a place for the interplay of signs and manuscripts which are non-totalizable. It is always a vain attempt to construct a totality out of manuscripts housed in an archive.

The library of the monastery is rhizomatic in that the very structure of the library is its structurelessness. It is an infinite space without centre, periphery or exit. This may also imply that it has too many centres, peripheries and exits, because of which, its structure cannot be stabilized or structured. This is a rhizomatic space defying linearity, causality and rationality, which paralyzes William's faculty of deduction, turning him from a Holmes-like detective monk to a postmodern one, relying no longer on rationality or underlying meaning of a sign and of the world, but on chance and surface connections without reason.

William is trapped in a rhizomatic archive housed not only the manuscript of Aristotle's second book of *Poetics*, whose subject is on comedy, but also Jorge of Burgos, the 'library's memory and the soul of the scriptorium' (130), who wants to conceal this manuscript, believing that 'laughter foments doubt' (132) and fearing that 'laughter is something very close to death and to the corruption of the body' (96) and that 'laughter shakes the body, distorts the features of the face, makes man similar to the monkey' (131). Jorge is described as an evil character and the most suitable place for him is the monastery's Piranesi-like evil library. This Spanish monk is portrayed as a criminal having 'a malignant mind brooding for a long time in darkness over a murderous plan' (265). He is blind but can orchestrate his plan to conceal Aristotle's manuscript. He murders others by lacing the manuscript with poison. On the one hand, he is hungry for knowledge and truth, and on the other, he is at pains to conceal the truth, which drives him into eating up the poisoned forbidden manuscript while the library is burning fiercely:

> His face, in the reddish glow of the lamp, now seemed horrible to us: the features were distorted, a malignant sweat streaked his brow and cheeks, his eyes, usually a deathly white, were bloodshot, from his mouth came scraps of parchment, and he looked like a ravening beast who had stuffed himself and could no longer swallow his food. Disfigured by anxiety, by the menace of the poison now flowing

> abundantly through his veins, by his desperate and diabolical determination, the venerable figure of the old man now seemed disgusting and grotesque. (483)

Jorge of Burgos now becomes a 'ravening beast' stuffing himself with scraps of manuscripts. His 'diabolical determination' to devour the forbidden text which is poisoned and poisoning turns him into a 'disgusting and grotesque' old man disfigured by anxiety. The apocalyptic tone of this consumption of paper is underscored by its allusion to the Book of Revelation (10:9–10):

> And I went unto the angel, and said unto him, Give me the little book. And he said unto me, Take it, and eat it up; and it shall make thy belly bitter, but it shall be in thy mouth sweet as honey.
>
> And I took the little book out of the angel's hand, and ate it up; and it was in my mouth sweet as honey: and as soon as I had eaten it, my belly was bitter. (King James version)

Jorge's consumption of the manuscript can be likened on the one hand to his desire for knowledge, his desire for preserving and at the same time concealing and preventing the dissemination of Aristotle's manuscript, and on the other, to the consumption of manuscripts of the library by fire. The library is feverish as its manuscripts are burning and turning into ashes. The novel begins with the Word but ends with ashes. Here, the permanence of writing is put into question. The destination or the destiny of writing is cinder which, as Derrida says, leaves only traceless traces (Derrida 1995, 391).

Jorge of Burgos, the evil blind Spanish librarian, is especially significant for the library, the archive and the manuscript. Eco states in his *Postscript to The Name of the Rose* that

> Everyone asks me why my Jorge, with his name, suggests Borges, and why Borges is so wicked. But I cannot say. I wanted a blind man who guarded a library (it seemed a good narrative idea to me), and library plus blind man can only equal Borges, also because debts must be paid. And, further, it was through Spanish commentaries and illumination that the Apocalypse influenced the entire Middle Ages. (Eco 1984, 27–8)

It is apparent that this Spanish monk Jorge of Burgos is Jorge Luis Borges, both of whom are blind librarians, spending most of their lives in the library. It is also obvious that Borges is an underlying figure of this novel. When writing this novel, Eco is already in Borges's memories and shadow, and has already inherited his memories. In order to pay debts to him, Eco immerses this novel of his with Borgesian (and also Latin American literary) topics – the library, the labyrinth and the manuscript. More is revealed on the archive through the confrontation between Jorge and William. On one level, the encounter between William and Jorge represents that this medieval Italian library is a rhizomatic site for the confrontation between rationality and irrationality, between good and evil, and between the desire to seek the truth and the attempt to conceal the truth.

On another level, their encountering each other also symbolizes the confrontation between a Sherlock Holmes deprived of the faculty of deduction and a Borgesian minotaur that devours anything entering its labyrinth. In the centre of this rhizomatic labyrinth is Borges the blind minotaur preserving and obliterating the forbidden text.

But what kind of debts is Eco paying to Borges? By turning him into an evil murderer and a blind guardian of the library, suffering from archive fever and eating up a manuscript of comedy, this is more like slighting than a debt paid to Borges. On the one hand, Eco turns Borges into a nasty character. Borges's playfulness with the text and the manuscript thus vanishes into thin air. Worse still, he becomes a manuscript-eater and a victim of his own contrivance – being burned to death in his own archive fever and gobbling up the manuscript that he has poisoned. On the other hand, Eco seems to stage an unconscious revenge on Borges for stealing, raiding the archive before him. Eco unconsciously reveals a European dislike for Argentine appropriation of the European archive.

Eco's medieval Italian library at the end feverishly burns itself into ashes, burning in its own archive fever:

> The Abbey burned for three days and three nights, and the last efforts were of no avail. As early as that morning of the seventh day of our sojourn in that place, when the survivors were fully aware that no building could be saved, when the finest constructions showed only their ruined outer walls, and the church, as if drawing into itself, swallowed its tower – even at that point everyone's will to combat the divine chastisement failed. (497)

God finishes his creation of the universe on the seventh day, but the abbey in the novel experiences utter destruction on the seventh day of William and Adso's sojourn – everything is burned into ashes, the distinction between the inside and the outside no longer holds, and the church seems to be swallowing its own tower. This is regarded as the divine chastisement. Borges's Library of Babel is similarly a burning and feverish one with books like a delirious divinity, and this Total Library and its Italian counterpart transcend each other in different ways. The rhizomatic labyrinth in *The Name of the Rose* is an archive without structure, centre or hierarchy, which defies definition and totalization, while the Library of Babel is paradoxically a chaotic yet orderly library – an orderly shelving system and identical hexagonal galleries consist of exact numbers of shelves of books but at the same time, books shelved are impenetrable, 'formless and chaotic' by nature with 'senseless cacophonies, verbal jumbles and incoherences' even in every sensible line of straightforward statement (80).

On the other hand, the total Library of Babel transcends its rhizomatic counterpart in that the latter is reduced to ashes by fire, by its own evil librarian. This medieval Italian library begins with the Word, with writing, with thousands of manuscripts in heterogeneous nature housed in it, but ends in ashes. This signifies the impermanence of writing and its destiny of becoming untraceable ashes. However, the Library of Babel will endure even upon the arrival of the apocalypse:

> I suspect that the human species – the unique species – is about to be extinguished, but the Library will endure: illuminated, solitary, infinite, perfectly motionless, equipped with precious volumes, useless, incorruptible, secret. (*Labyrinths*, 1964, 85)

and can last even after human races are extinguished. It is as incorruptible, enduring and capacious as Funes' indelible memory, and at the same time, they are both useless. A mysterious unnamed editor at the very end of 'The Library of Babel' says,

> Letizia Álvarez de Toledo has observed that this vast Library is useless: rigorously speaking, *a single volume* would be sufficient, a volume of ordinary format, printed in nine or ten point type, containing an infinite number of infinitely thin leaves. (86) (original italics)

Both Funes' memory and the total library are useless yet capacious, housing indelible memories and books. In this sense, Funes is not simply an inhabitant in this Library of Babel, or its librarian, but the library itself. The uselessness of Funes' memories and of this total library lies in its defiance to generalization, categorization and territorialization, and it is because of this uselessness that Funes' memory and the total library become infinitely large. But what is the point of stressing this uselessness? The answer may be that Borges is raiding the archive by stretching the concept of the archive and the manuscript beyond imagination. That is why his archive is all-encompassing, incorruptible, infinite yet impenetrable, solitary and useless.

There is a strong intertextual, translational and colonial relationship among Cervantes, Borges and Eco around the theme of the archive. Borges replies to Cervantes by translating Cervantes' Don Quixote and Glass Graduate into Funes like a mirror repeating but at the same time, reversing the same image. Don Quixote and the Glass Graduate's archive created by knight-errantry as writing is now turned into Funes' archive of memory as useless yet enduring as the Library of Babel. Borges is then translated and raided by Eco, who not only turns him into a diabolical librarian, but also makes his labyrinth rhizomatic. Borges inherits Cervantes' memories and is in Cervantes' shadow, but goes beyond it by his playfulness, while Eco is always in the shadow of Borges, paying debts to him in the form of slighting.

The archive in these works is a place to get lost. Both Don Quixote and the Glass Graduate lose their sanity and hence their bearings in society. Funes is paralyzed and loses his subjectivity and direction in his memory. William loses his deductive faculty in the rhizomatic library and Jorge of Burgos loses his life by consuming the very book that he is at pains to preserve and conceal. These characters are inflicted with the evil of the archive, manifested in the form of violence and trauma. This evil of the archive destroys them during the process of its self-destruction. Don Quixote and the Glass Graduate become repressive and insane and hence need to create a reality in which their life will become bearable and meaningful. This is reversed by Borges. The reality Funes has forged is the one which is unbearably excessive, and this causes both his lung and mental congestions. He writes in the form of memory and his archive and reality are full of memories as manuscripts. The reality in which the confrontation between William and Jorge is staged is a rhizomatic structure without structure, and one inevitably gets lost in such a centreless and structureless archive, in which manuscripts abound but the exit is no where in sight.

The progression from Cervantes to Borges and then to Eco, from Spain to Argentina and then to Italy, seems to be a regressive one – from a bearable and idealistic reality created out of a world that is going or gone, to an unbearable reality excessive with useless heap of memories, and then to a rhizomatic reality. One is bound to get lost and drawn into the centre of the archive by its regressive force. While Borges raids and unpacks the library, Puig playfully unsettles the archives of the discourse on homosexuality, the Hollywood movies and the police records through the spider woman.

Chapter 6
Puig:
Dialogue with the Spider Woman

MINISTRY OF THE INTERIOR OF THE ARGENTINE REPUBLIC
Penitentiary of the City of Buenos Aires
Report to the Warden, prepared by Staff Assistants
Prisoner 3018, Luis Alberto Molina
Sentenced July 20, 1974, by the Honorable Judge Justo José Dalpierre, Criminal Court of the City of Buenos Aires. Condemned to eight years imprisonment for …
Detainee 16115, Valentin Arregui Paz
Arrested October 16, 1972, along Route 5, outside Barrancas, National Guard troops having surrounded group of activists involved …

Puig[1]

Do not ask who I am and do not ask me to remain the same: leave it to our bureaucrats and our police to see that our papers are in order.

Foucault[2]

Puig's *Kiss of the Spider Woman* shares certain features with the feminine texts of *The Arabian Nights* and Cervantes' 'The Dialogue of the Dogs' and *Don Quixote* in that the momentum of the narrative is motivated, generated and propelled by a seductive narrator and the power of narrative seduction. Like the reincarnation of the Glass Graduate in Ireneo Funes in Borges's 'Funes the Memorious', Cervantes' shadow can be found in *Kiss of the Spider Woman.* This chapter focuses on the feminine character of Molina's seductive narrative, on how the archive in the forms of the police records, the Hollywood movies and the discourse on homosexuality is destabilized. Another focus of this chapter is the impossibility of telling in an archive.

6.1. Molina as Seductive Narrator

Luis Alberto Molina is a narrator like Scheherazade and Cañizares. Molina is like Scheherazade, who narrates her stories at night in the form of seduction so as to entertain, to draw the listener into the labyrinth of her interpolating texts,

---

1 Manuel Puig, *Kiss of the Spider Woman*, trans. Thomas Colchie (New York: Vintage Books, 1979), p. 148, (originally published in Spanish as *El Beso de la Mujer Arana* in 1976).

2 Michel Foucault, *The Archaeology of Knowledge and The Discourse on Language* trans. Sheridan Smith (New York: Pantheon Books, 1972), p. 17.

and above all, to fend off and delay death. He is also like Cañizares, who seduces Berganza into the story of not only his biography, but also hers. Molina, a homosexual who views himself as a woman, unfolds his film stories at night to entertain Valentin Arregui Paz in an unnamed prison in Buenos Aires between 4 April to 8 October 1975. In his story telling, he plays the role of a seductive woman as narrator. But unlike Scheherazade, Molina's story-telling is motivated by a complicated, multi-layered intention. His story-telling at first glance is a means to entertain his cellmate Valentin so as to make himself less depressed in his prison cell. This is a way of distraction so that they can temporarily as well as mentally escape from the harsh and tedious reality of their confinement in prison:

> Well, it's just that the film was divine, and for me that's what counts, because I'm locked up in this cell and I'm better off thinking about nice things, so I don't go nuts, see? … Well?
>
> What do you want me to say?
>
> That you'll let me escape from reality once in a while, because why should I let myself get more depressed than I am? (78)

Molina is a storyteller never short of stories to tell. His memory of film stories is as archivally rich as Funes'. He believes that telling these film stories is a way to keep his sanity and to avoid going nuts. They are 'nice things' and 'divine' as through them he can 'escape from reality', even though it is only 'once in a while'. To Molina, films have a transcending power and can lift him out of his unpleasant world. But Valentin thinks otherwise, believing these 'nice things' can be dangerous:

> No, be serious, it's true you can end up going nuts in this place, but you can drive yourself crazy here in other ways, not just out of despair … but from alienating yourself the way you do. Because that business of only thinking about nice things, as you put it, well, that can be dangerous too.
>
> How? I don't think so.
>
> It can become a vice, always trying to escape from reality like that, it's like taking drugs or something. Because, listen to me, reality, I mean *your reality*, isn't restricted by this cell we live in. If you read something, if you study something, you transcend any cell you're inside of, do you understand what I'm saying? That's why I read and why I study every day. (78) (original ellipsis and italics)

Ironically, these nice things regarded as drugs by Valentin are what he gets addicted to at the end. As he gets deeper and deeper into the labyrinthine narrative of Molina, he demands more and more and urges Molina to tell him more – 'Go ahead. I want to know what happens' (231), 'Why are you stopping?' (232), 'Tell me a little before it's time to go to sleep' (236), 'I'm listening, go ahead' (238), 'Don't stop' (240) and such urges, commands and demands are getting more and more frequent at the end of the novel, especially in the last film story that Molina narrates. Valentin is desiring for an endless story, a narrative which will continue without stopping, and this is like what Sancho Panza asks for from Don Quixote.

Valentin's addiction to Molina's seductive narrative shows not only how successful and skillful Molina is in his narrating, but also the power of such a seductive narrative woven by a narrator whose gender is in question. Molina represents a destabilization of patriarchal discourse in terms of sexuality. He is a man as a woman and also metaphorically a woman as a man. His narrative in this regard is a feminine power and a homosexual discourse contesting patriarchy, which shows that there is a discourse which is non-patriarchal.

Like Don Quixote, who attempts to create his reality out of the imaginary by means of knight-errantry, Molina, collaborating with Valentin, embarks on a similar undertaking, but this time, by re-telling sentimental Hollywood 'B' movies. Through his film stories, Molina successfully creates a reality, which not only draws Valentin into the archive of Molina's narrative, but also ignites Valentin's emotions, resulting in a metamorphosis in Valentin and surprisingly in Molina as well. Molina's film stories in this regard are to seduce and to draw Valentin into his narrative, his erotic desire and his homosexuality. At the same time, Valentin's emotions and his desire for narrative are aroused. This reveals a number of implications. On one level, movie going is implied as a feminine pursuit, as exemplified by the homosexual Molina, in contrast with politics, which is depicted as a masculine enterprise founded upon the heterosexual family unit, as represented by the revolutionary Valentin.[3] So, the juxtaposition here is film narrative as a feminine pursuit and politics as a masculine undertaking. Films are both seductive and feminizing, and this complements the hegemonic masculine politics and ideology. Film narrative is seductive because it is on the side of the erotic, and it is feminizing as it encourages passivity and paradoxically, it also disarms the rational grip of ideological hegemony and patriarchal institution by arousing desire and accentuating pleasure.

The contrast between Molina and Valentin at the beginning of the novel, in this light, can be viewed as the differences between films and politics. Thirty-seven-year-old Molina is homosexual and apolitical, while twenty-six-year-old Valentin is heterosexual, rational and revolutionary ('There's no way I can live for the moment, because my life is dedicated to political struggle, or, you know, political action, let's call it.') (27); Molina is passive and sensual, while Valentin is active and intellectual; Molina plays the role of a feminine narrator while Valentin is a masculine listener; Molina takes care of Valentin as a surrogate mother when he has eaten poisoned food, while Valentin in such a relationship is a dependent son:

---

[3] As pointed out by Stacey Olster in *The Trash Phenomenon: Contemporary Literature, Popular Culture, and the Making of the American Century*, Chapter 5 'Flotsam and Peronism in the Novels of Manuel Puig', p. 103 (Athens and London: The University of Georgia Press, 2003).

> Well, I could help you clean yourself. Look, we can heat some water up in the pot, we already have two towels, so one we soap up and you wash the front of yourself, I can do the back for you, and with the other towel slightly wet we sponge off the soap.
>
> And then my body wouldn't itch so much?
>
> That's right, we can do it bit by bit, so you don't catch any chill, first your neck and ears, then your underarms, then your arms, your chest, your back, and so on.
>
> And you'd really help me?
>
> Obviously. (179–80)

Molina offers maternal care to Valentin and very gently cleans his body 'bit by bit', while Valentin reacts and responds like a child, seeking reassurance that his body will not be itchy and that he can sleep peacefully after the wash. Molina becomes the mother capturing Valentin's body and affection, while Valentin becomes the son being taken care of by Molina.

Another contrast between Molina and Valentin is that Molina represents the will to pleasure, while Valentin the will to knowledge. In the daytime, Molina is a caring mother, taking pleasure in nursing the body of Valentin, but at night, the seductive power of his narration of film stories turns his motherly love into an erotic one. The daytime is for this dependent son Valentin's political reading, silent study and intellectual pursuit, while at night, he gradually succumbs to Molina's seduction, first verbally through the web of narrative and the archive of Hollywood films, and then physically through the caress of Molina.

6.2. *Don Quixote* Recast

Molina's narrative in the form of film stories, on another level, implies its destabilizing power to undo the boundary and territory of sexuality. Molina's destabilizing power is especially accentuated in that, he is right at the beginning of the novel a marginalized homosexual, but now he is a powerful and skillful storyteller. He is the reincarnation of not only Scheherazade, but also Cervantes' witch Cañizares in 'The Dialogue of the Dogs', both of whom are most powerful when narrating. Outside the prison, he is a powerless and victimized figure under the weight of ideological and patriarchal repression. But Molina exercises his power most fully upon Valentin within the bare walls of a prison, which is a space of panoptical surveillance, claustrophobic confinement and above all, intense centralization of silencing institution and hence an oppressive but invisible presence of insidious death. A marginalized effeminate homosexual now seduces and hence manipulates his cellmate. He is powerful only when he is in prison, only at nighttime and only in narrating. In other words, it is within the prison cell, which symbolizes the strongest patriarchal suppression, and within his own narration that his narrative seduction is most effective. It reveals that narration can be liberating and that seduction can be a form of liberation. If so, Valentin's imprisonment is paradoxical. He is physically imprisoned in the prison and at the same time, he is liberated in Molina's seductive narrative. Or the liberation by Molina's seductive film stories functions to resist the physical imprisonment of the prison cell. This implies Molina and Valentin's temporary escapism is attained through the liberating and seductive narrative from a 'male' narrator in a feminine voice.

Puig actually is questioning, writing and raiding the archive through a feminine figure. Molina is in a manipulating position because of his seductive narration. By his seductive narrating of film stories, he attempts to achieve what he wants – on the one hand, he uses Valentin and especially the information on Valentin's comrades to get his freedom; and on the other hand, he uses the police warden to win Valentin's trust, affection and body and finally to have sex with him. This does not mean that Valentin is turned into a homosexual. Molina's undoing of sexuality does not mean to turn heterosexuality into homosexuality, to turn every heterosexual he encounters into a homosexual. It only means that by the seductive power of his narrative, Molina manages successfully to blur the boundary of heterosexuality and to expand the realm of homosexuality – his homosexuality upon Valentin's heterosexuality. It first means that one manifestation of patriarchal archive is heterosexuality, which is constructed by patriarchy and which Molina tries to undo. Second, Molina functions as a raider of this archive of sexuality by being playful with it, de-territorializing its limit and blurring its boundary. As seen from Valentin, who is at the end willing to sleep with Molina, the sexual becomes neither hetero nor homo. Sexuality can no longer be polarized rigidly as either hetero or homo. But this destabilization of sexuality has to begin with its own self first. Before Molina destabilizes Valentin's sexuality, he has to destabilize his own, by turning himself into a marginalized homosexual repressed by the patriarchal ideology. Before he seduces Valentin into having sex with him, he is first seduced and attracted by him.

Like the way he unsettles and blurs sexuality, Molina, through his narration of film stories, undoes identity, especially Valentin's. Valentin gradually becomes a dependent son in need of Molina's maternal care and caress, and surrenders his body to him. He loses his subjectivity and identity during Molina's narration, and finally, he and Molina become one:

> And know what else I felt, Valentin? But only for a second, no more.
> What? Talk to me, but just … don't move …
> For just a second, it seemed like I wasn't there … not here or anywhere out there either …
> …
> It seemed as if I wasn't here at all … like it was you all alone.
> …
> Or like I wasn't me anymore. As if now, somehow … I … were you.
> (219) (original ellipses)

Molina and Valentin escape not only their spatial location, but also their own identities. The concepts of spatiality, subjectivity and identity are no longer of any importance when they become one in both their sexual intercourse and the seductive narrative of the film stories. On one level, it is without doubt that Molina is transformed into a revolutionary and that Valentin is converted into not simply a homosexual, but a heterosexual who enlarges, plays with his heterosexuality. Valentin's attachment to Molina's seductive narrative is like Sancho Panza's attachment to Don Quixote's knight-errantry. In the former, there is a mutual dependency between the listener and the storyteller, the narratee and the narrator, while in the latter, such a mutual dependency is manifested in the form of a knight-squire, master-servant relationship. This knight-squire relationship between Don Quixote and Sancho Panza gradually turns into a process of identity switching. In the second part of the novel, Sancho Panza becomes less of a servant or squire, but more of a partner. At the end, both of them affect each other so deeply that they see life differently from their previous selves, which results in the 'Quixotization' of Sancho Panza and the 'Sanchification' of Don Quixote.[4] Sancho Panza rises from a position of pragmatic reality to the dream of idealistic pursuit, and conversely, Don Quixote descends from his idealistic dream to a pragmatic reality.

The relationship between Molina and Valentin, however, is much more complicated. Besides the 'Molinization' of Valentin and the 'Valentinization' of Molina, their narrator-listener relationship becomes an erotic one between two males created out of seductive narrative. Both Molina and Valentin create their reality which helps them survive their unbearable reality. But the difference is that their reality is craved and generated out of feminizing yet liberating film discourse. The Molinization that Valentin undergoes does lead him to a realm of homo-eroticism, and the Valentinization that Molina experiences does pull him to the side of politics, but both of them still immerse themselves in the world of seductive narrative. Their destabilization of identities comes from narrative seduction; and the more their identities are destabilized, the deeper the seductive narrative they immerse. Puig is recasting *Don Quixote*, especially the relationship between Don Quixote and Sancho Panza, and raiding Cervantes' archive by sexualizing such a relationship.

6.3. Archives Fictionalized

The source of Molina's destabilizing power comes from the film stories that he narrates, re-produces and re-interprets. The six film stories that Molina narrates accentuate and blend not only love and politics, but also fantasy and violence together. They can be summarized as follows:

---

4 The ideas of 'Sanchification' of Quixote and 'Quixotification' of Sancho are from Salvador de Madariaga's *Don Quixote: An introductory essay in psychology* (London: Geoffrey Cumberledge, 1948), discussed by Anthony Close in *The Romantic Approach to 'Don Quixote'* (Cambridge: Cambridge University Press, 1977), pp. 102 and 141.

Chapters 1 and 2: the panther woman (*Cat People*, 1942), which is about a dilemma between erotic desire and violence
Chapters 3 and 4: an imaginary Nazi propaganda film with a plot of romance and political conspiracy
Chapter 5: *The Enchanted Cottage* (1944), which is a sentimental love story about a plain girl and a disfigured man
Chapter 6: an invented film concerning political conversion and a family romance
Chapters 9 to 11: a horror film *I Walked with a Zombie* (1943), with a fantastic and sentimental plot of love, murder and mystery, a modern Caribbean version of *Jane Eyre*
Chapters 12 to 14: a fabricated romantic tragedy set in Mexico[5]

To both Molina and Valentin, these six films are not only a source of pleasure, but also a source of liberation. Their blatant effect is a reconciliation of differences between Molina and Valentin and a destabilization of their identity and sexuality. These films consist of both genuine and invented ones. What Puig is doing is to question the archive, by mingling true manuscripts with the fake ones to blur textuality, and to see the possibility of turning the archive into fiction. Molina's film stories can be taken as the archive of Hollywood 'B' movies, in which these Hollywood movies are always colonizing. This is a postcolonial response to the colonizer – using his devices to overthrow his domination. By inserting a fictional film among the true ones, the authenticity and authority of the Hollywood archive become questionable.

Perhaps, Valentin's responses to Molina's film stories can be regarded as violent interruptions by which Valentin takes Molina away from his privileged place by interrupting his narration.[6] However, if this is so, such narrative interruptions will not lead to reconciliation of differences, let alone the development of intimate relationship between Molina and Valentin. In the absence of an omniscient narrator, Valentin is drawn into Molina's seductive narrative by being a co-narrator, commenting on the film stories, discussing with Molina not only these stories, but also their implications, and above all, urging him to carry on with his narration. Unlike Scheherazade who narrates her stories alone, in fear of being put to death in case her stories fail to seduce and capture her listener's attention, now Molina and Valentin are partners in propelling their seductive narrative forward. Instead of a narrator-narratee relationship, there are two narrators in the prison. In this light, Valentin does not create any destructive violence against Molina's narration.

---

5 From Lucille Kerr's *Suspended Fictions: Reading Novels by Manuel Puig* (Urbana and Chicago: University of Illinois Press, 1987), p. 193. Pamela Bacarisse also gives a detailed discussion on these films told by Molina in *The Necessary Dream: A Study of the Novels of Manuel Puig* (Totowa, NJ: Barnes and Noble Books, 1988), Chapter 5: 'The Kiss of Death': El beso de la mujer araña (1976), pp. 86–125.

6 As discussed in Lucille Kerr's *Suspended Fictions: Reading Novels by Manuel Puig* (Urbana and Chicago: University of Illinois Press, 1987), pp. 197–8.

On the contrary, he unconsciously becomes a positive force driving Molina's seductive narrative forwards. Molina is not a lone spider weaving her own web of seductive narrative and Valentin is not simply his prey, but shares an important part in his narration. Valentin's indispensable role in Molina's narration can be likened to the typographical blank spaces '…' found in various places in the novel, especially in and after the love scene between Molina and Valentin:

> Don't talk, Molina … for a little while.
> It's that I … I feel such strange things …
> …
> Just then, without thinking, I put my hand up to my face, trying to find the mole.
> What mole? … I have it, not you.
> Mmm, I know. But I put my hand to my forehead, to feel the mole that … I haven't got.
> …
> It looks so handsome on you, it's a shame … why can't I see you?
> …
> Are you enjoying it, Valentin?
> Just quiet … just quiet a little while.
> …
> …
> And know what else I felt, Valentin? But only for a second, no more.
> What? Talk to me, but just … don't move …
> For just a second, it seemed like I wasn't here … not here or anywhere out there either …
> …
> It seemed as if I wasn't here at all … like it was you all alone.
> …
> Or like I wasn't me anymore. As if now, somehow … I … were you.
> (219) (original ellipses)

These blank spaces allow various interpretations. They are like the unconscious of Molina and Valentin. They are ellipses by which what should be revealed is concealed. They can also be gaps or interstices where identity is erased. But at the same time, they can be invitations. They invite the reader to be a co-author and to take active participation in completing the narrative.[7] If so, these blank spaces are not simply silence or concealment, but interstices for the reader's creativity, participation and interpretation. Far from obstructing the flow of the narrative, these blank spaces are conducive to the momentum of the narrative, which is what Valentin is functioning in Molina's narration.

The real violence against Molina's narrative and also against the plot of the novel comes from the footnotes. There are all together nine footnotes to the main text of the novel. These footnotes are mainly on homosexuality and repression

---

[7] This is discussed in *Manuel Puig* by Jonathan Tittler (New York: Twayne Publishers, 1993), p. 61.

by various scholars and other authoritative sources: D.J. West in Chapters 3 and 5; a press-book entitled *Her Real Glory* from Tobis-Berlin Studios in Chapter 4; T.C.N. Gibbons and C.S. Lewis in Chapter 5; Sigmund Freud in Chapters 5 to 7; Anna Freud in Chapter 6; O. Fenichel in Chapter 7; and some more authoritative voices in footnotes in Chapters 9 and 10. These footnotes simultaneously link with and separate from the main text of the novel. Puig is actually offering and at the same time raiding an archive on homosexuality. These 'authoritative' discourses on homosexuality are ironically marginalized as footnotes lying below the fictional plot of the novel. The centre is fiction while these authoritative discourses of sociology and psychology are situated on the margin. If homosexuality is regarded as the 'other' discourse, now these 'authoritative' discourses on the otherness become the other to the fictional narrative at the centre. Before these authoritative discourses effect their marginalization, they are first marginalized in the novel, which is parallel to Molina's seduction – to seduce Valentin because he is in the first place attracted towards him.

These footnotes are like manuscripts as it is never certain who narrates them. They are thus non-attributable and non-originating, further unsettling the authority of their own discourse on homosexuality. These footnotes are paradoxical in that they constitute the archive of homosexuality, but they are like manuscripts – liberating, non-attributable and non-originating.

Within these authoritative discourses, one interesting point is the existence of an invented fictional 'authoritative' scholar in the last footnote in Chapter 11, named Anneli Taube. This fictional Danish doctor, together with the summary of his non-existent text *Sexuality and Revolution*, unsettles textuality and the polyphonic interplay of the authoritative voices in the previous footnotes. García Márquez's *Chronicle of a Death Foretold*, reverses this – a fictional account of a real murder committed on 22 January 1951 in Sucre, Bolivia, in which there are García Márquez's own parents, his four younger siblings and even his then wife-to-be Mercedes as informants among other fictional characters (which will be discussed in the next chapter). In *Kiss of the Spider Woman*, the presence of a fictional text within the footnotes accentuates not only the destabilization of textuality and of these authoritative discourses, but also their heterogeneity, which ironically includes both the real and the fictional. This leads to the question of how true these authoritative discourses are. Puig is raiding this archive on homosexuality by inserting a fictional manuscript written by himself. Like the six films discussed, these footnotes containing both real and fictional discourse are only to show the impossibility of telling in the archive, and more importantly, the impossibility of telling the truth.

This problematization of the archive can be seen from the implicit references to the police archive in the novel.[8] Chapter 8 of *Kiss of the Spider Woman* begins with a short police report, giving factual information about the two protagonists

[8] Philip Swanson in *The new novel in Latin America: Politics and popular culture after the Boom* (Manchester and New York: Manchester University Press, 1995), Chapter 2, pp. 35–6, points out the treacherous nature of discourse revealed in the police reports. These reports suggesting official discourse, authority and power are now pervaded by uncertainty,

from the police's point of view. This can be regarded as another 'authoritative' patriarchal discourse on its subjects, who are deviant in terms of the sexual and the political. The full names of the two protagonists – Luis Alberto Molina and Valentin Arregui Paz, are revealed only in this police report, with their middle names indicated for archival documentation and identification, and with their prisoner numbers and backgrounds. The police archive is the place for hoarding such information.

It is surprising that such an archival document is 'prepared by Staff Assistants' (148). If it is written and prepared by some unknown, unspecified 'Staff Assistants', there is no way of tracing the authenticity and the source of the details on the report, in case queries arise. This reveals the contradiction that such an authoritative police document is non-attributable. Furthermore, this 'authoritative' police report is followed immediately by a dialogue between the police agents (the guard and the warden) and the prisoner (Molina). This dialogue destabilizes the authority of the report, as Molina at the end successfully (although temporarily) gets extra food and groceries and delays the police's investigation of Valentin by being part of it. Chapter 15 is another police report on Molina after his release. In this report, Molina is deprived of his 'proper' name and is mentioned as the 'subject', which is true in that he is always the 'subject' of patriarchy, whether inside or outside the prison. It is only in his own narrative that he is the subject of his own self. This report from the police archive details the whereabouts of Molina and what he does outside the prison, giving a strong sense of police surveillance even outside the prison. This implies that the freedom Molina enjoys outside the prison is only fictitious. This police document ends with the death of Molina. It seems that in the eye of the patriarchal police force, each individual's life is only a document in their archive – beginning with his offence or crime and ending with his release or death. Molina is most alive in his seductive, liberating narrative, and in his own archive forged by his own narrative. The very end of this police document reads:

> The present compilation of reports has been typed up in quadruplicate, for distribution only to authorized personnel, with the original to remain in this office permanently on file. (274)

Puig seems to respond to González Echevarría's definition of the archive – origin, secrecy and power, as discussed in Chapter 1. Now, this 'original' report on Molina will be shelved permanently in the police archive, kept as a secret and accessible only to 'authorized personnel'. But the idea of origin in the archive is mocked here by the four duplicates of the report. As Freud mentions in 'The Uncanny' that the existence of the copy only knocks down the idea of the origin.[9] With the collapse

---

e.g., the transcript of the Warden's telephone conversation displays an inability to interpret Molina's actions.

[9] Freud, 'The Uncanny' in *The Standard Edition of The Complete Psychological Works of Sigmund Freud, Vol. XVII (1917–1919): An Infantile Neurosis and Other Works*, trans. James Strachey (London: Vintage, 1955), p. 235.

of the idea of the origin in the archive comes the archive's inability not only to tell, but also to tell the truth and the questionable existence of truth. If so, this is an archive turned into a fiction.

Puig writes in Cervantes' shadow, playfully turning Cervantes' Cañizares into Molina, and playfully sexualizing the knight-squire relationship between Don Quixote and Sancho Panza. Puig raids the archive through a feminine figure. Molina represents not only a castrating female, but also a male fantasy. Like Cañizares, who is good at tropelía, he unsettles the authenticity of the archive of the Hollywood 'B' movies by inserting a fictional film story in it. His presence not only upsets patriarchal authority by having a woman disguised as a man, or vice versa, to be the narrator, but also destabilizes sexuality, textuality and authenticity. *Don Quixote* is recast, sexualized through Molina's seductive narrative and the co-authorship of Molina and Valentin for this manuscript. Don Quixote creates his reality through knight-errantry, through an exploration of the imaginary past so as to transform the present oppressive and alienating reality into an idealistic one; likewise, Molina and Valentin co-found their fluid reality out of film stories in which all that is solid is undone. Territory can no longer be territorialized, identity cannot be stabilized and sexuality can hardly be fixed. Although Molina and Valentin cannot decide how they die, this powerful seductive narrative offers them another chance, a second opportunity to get out of their labyrinth of solitude. The archive is raided and liberated through the presence of fictional texts in Molina's film discourse and in the footnotes, which results in the revelation of the impossibility of telling, especially the impossibility of telling the truth in the archive.

What Puig is doing is raiding and writing three archives at once – the police archive, the archive of homosexuality and the archive of the Hollywood 'B' movies. The police report in the police archive is made non-attributable and non-originating. The archive of homosexuality is marginalized to be the footnotes to the main text. Its authority is taken away and undone by the presence of a discourse written by a fictional scholar. Furthermore, its attributability is in question as it is no longer sure who narrates these footnotes. These footnotes, in this regard, are manuscripts in disguise. The archive of the Hollywood 'B' movies is problematized by the feminine marginalized narrator who not only changes it, but also presents a fictional one. He plays with this archive and makes use of it for his enjoyment and purpose.

Puig's raiding of Cervantes' archive, through the homosexual figure Molina, stresses the seductive yet liberating discourse of the feminine text within a paralyzing and homogenizing archive. García Márquez follows this and turns Cervantes into a brothel owner and prostitute María Alejandrina Cervantes in *Chronicle of a Death Foretold*, raiding the archive by exposing its impossibility to have a plot within a story. This is the focus of the next chapter.

Chapter 7
García Márquez: Archives and Manuscripts

Cervantes' archive is turned by Borges from a utopian reality forged out of the imaginary to an unbearable one with excessive memory, and Puig raids the archives of patriarchy through a feminine seductive narrator Molina. García Márquez adds a carnivalesque touch to the archive so as to turn it into a new kind of utopia. In his *Chronicle of a Death Foretold*,[1] Miguel de Cervantes Saavedra is feminized and turned into a brothel owner María Alejandrina Cervantes. She is a strong allusion to Rojas' Celestina, Cervantes' witch Cañizares in 'The Dialogue of Dogs', and the Moorish woman in 'The Glass Graduate', all of whom being female destabilizing agents.

The plot of this novella is as follows: Bayardo San Roman, an attractive, rich young man, shows up in August at an unnamed small town, in an attempt to seek a wife. Angela Vicario catches his fancy. At first, she resists him but is eventually talked into marrying him by her parents. A wedding feast is held six months later. On the night of their wedding, however, Bayardo returns Angela to her family because he discovers that she is not a virgin. Brutally interrogated by her mother as to the culprit, Angela mentions Santiago Nasar, the only son of an Arab family. In revenge, her twin brothers Pedro and Pablo murder Santiago with machetes in front of his house before the eyes of most people. After three years' imprisonment, the twins are acquitted on the grounds of justifiable homicide, Bayardo leaves the town, and Angela suddenly falls in love with him. For the next 17 years, she writes a weekly letter to her 'husband', who one August day shows up with her 2,000 letters, unopened, and says, 'Well, here I am'.[2]

But is it really possible to summarise the plot of this novella? Is there a sjuzet for the fabula, to put it in terms of Russian Formalism? Vladimir Propp and Tzvetan Todorov distinguish the 'fabula', that is, the content or the story, from the 'sjuzet', that is, the way the fabula is told, or the plot.[3] In other words,

---

1 *Chronicle of a Death Foretold* by Gabriel García Márquez, trans. Gregory Rabassa (Harmondsworth: Penguin Books, 1982). Original Spanish title: *Cronica de una muerte anunciada* in which 'anunciada' can also mean 'annunciation'. This alludes to the Annunciation of the Virgin Mary by archangel Gabriel in Luke 1.26–38 about the birth of Jesus.

2 The crime to which this novella alludes occurred on Monday, 22 January 1951 in the town of Sucre, where García Márquez's family had lived for 10 years. For the details of this crime, see Gene Bell-Villada's *García Márquez: The Man and His Work* (Chapel Hill and London: The University of North Carolina Press, 1990), pp. 189–90.

3 See *Morphology of the Folktale* by Vladimir Propp, trans. Laurence Scott (Austin: University of Texas Press, 1968) and *The Poetics of Prose* by Tzvetan Todorov,

'fabula' refers to the preliterary, raw materials while 'sjuzet' is the way these raw materials are patterned, conveyed and represented. In this light, 'fabula' can be likened to a signified and 'sjuzet' to a signifier. It is worth noting that the novella ends with 2,000 letters. First, they are written by a woman to a man, which implies that they belong to a woman's archive, not to a patriarchal one. Second, they are unopened. It is never sure why they are unopened, but this reveals that the contents of these letters are kept unknowable, no matter how many letters are received. Like fabula and sjuzet, the letter and its content can be regarded as the signifier and the signified. Bayardo has got too many signifiers without knowing their signifieds respectively. On another level, the presence of these unopened letters may also mirror the structure of this novella – the fabula is still unknowable although many sjuzets have been attempted. In this regard, this is a story in which a plot cannot be established. This is a story without a plot.

The focus of this chapter is on *Chronicle of a Death Foretold* as a fabula in which it is impossible to have a sjuzet. It begins with a discussion of how Cervantes is rewritten into a carnivalised and grotesque figure of María Alejandrina Cervantes, and ends with a scrutiny of the carnivalesque and utopian elements of this archive which fails to give a narrative.

7.1. Cervantes Reincarnated

María Alejandrina Cervantes symbolizes bodily gratification and hedonism. As the owner of a brothel, she

> ... would only go to sleep once and that would be to die, was the most elegant and the most tender woman I have ever known, and the most serviceable in bed, but she was also the most strict. ... It was she who did away with my generation's virginity. She taught us much more than we should have learned, but she taught us above all that there's no place in life sadder than an empty bed. Santiago Nasar lost his senses the first time he saw her. I warned him: '*A falcon who chases a warlike crane can only hope for a life of pain.*' But he didn't listen to me, dazzled by María Alejandrina Cervantes' illusory calls. She was his mad passion, his mistress of tears at the age of fifteen, until Ibrahim Nasar [Santiago's father] drove him out of the bed with a whip and shut him up for more than a year on The Divine Face. (65–6) (original italics)

While the whole novella centres on the cult of virginity and the cult of honour, which ultimately lead to the death of Santiago Nasar, María Alejandrina Cervantes represents a destabilizing agent who undoes this generation's virginity.[4] Like Rojas'

---

trans. Richard Howard (Ithaca, New York: Cornell University Press, 1977). See also *Narrative and Ideology* by Jeremy Tambling (Milton Keynes and Philadelphia: Open University Press, 1991), especially pp. 26–7.

4 For more details on the cults of honour and virginity, see Arnold M. Penuel 'The Sleep of Vital Reason in García Márquez's *Cronica de una muerte anunciada*' in *Critical Essays on Gabriel García Márquez* ed. George R. McMurray (Boston: G.K. Hall and Co,

Celestina, Cervantes' Cañizares in 'The Dialogue of the Dogs' and the mysterious Moorish woman in 'The Glass Graduate', María Alejandrina Cervantes seems to have a witch-like magical power. She never sleeps or does not need to sleep. She sleeps only once, which is on the day when she dies. She is likened to a 'warlike crane' for a life of pain, able to give out illusory calls to dazzle Santiago Nasar when he is at the age of 15 and thus she becomes his 'mistress of tears'. With her illusory calls, she is not only a witch-like woman, but also a siren, luring and capturing Santiago Nasar and hence his death is implied as his inevitable fate.

María Alejandrina Cervantes' witch-like power of seduction also makes the narrator unconscious of what he does in her room:

> María Alejandrina Cervantes had left the door of the house unbarred. I took leave of my brother, crossed the veranda where the mulatto girls' cats were sleeping curled up among the tulips, and opened the bedroom door without knocking. The lights were out, but as soon as I went in I caught the smell of a warm woman and I saw the eyes of an insomniac leopard in the darkness, and then I didn't know anything else about myself until the bells began to ring. (69)

Whether the narrator's unconsciousness is real or fake, he loses his subjectivity under María Alejandrina Cervantes' witch-like seductive power manifested through the 'eyes of an insomniac leopard in the darkness'. This leopard's insomnia symbolizes both María Alejandrina Cervantes' power of resisting sleep and her power of seduction. This leopard is not only insomniac, but also sexually promiscuous, as the one Dante encounters in *Inferno* Canto I, when he is on his way to climb a hill after leaving the dark wood:

> Beyond the point the slope begins to rise
> Sprang up a leopard, trim and very swift!
> It was covered by a pelt of many spots. (Canto I, ll. 31–3)

This leopard represents lust or sexual promiscuity and likewise, María Alejandrina Cervantes' has lustful eyes of an insomniac leopard.

There are cleverly done multiple allusions in the name 'María Alejandrina Cervantes'. 'María', conspicuously, represents the motherly care and tenderness celebrated in the Catholic Church, while 'Alejandrina' is the feminine equivalent of 'Alexander', alluding to Alexander the Great and hence referring to the Hellenistic civilization. But Alexander the Great is now feminized. Her surname Cervantes, as mentioned above, alludes to Miguel de Cervantes, who represents the highest literary accomplishment of the Hispanic civilization, and who is also feminized. If María Alejandrina Cervantes now becomes a figure of a siren making illusory calls to lure and destroy the other, this may imply that the Catholic Church, the Hellenistic civilization and the works of Miguel de Cervantes are only

1987), especially pp. 189–94, in which the cult of virginity is related to the cult of death, and p. 198 in which María Alejandrina Cervantes is regarded as a symbol of fertility and the fullness of life.

illusory calls. They are only illusory representations or mimesis. Whether this is true or not, Miguel de Cervantes now becomes a beautiful but dangerous, magical yet lustful woman. Being a prostitute, she represents a liminal figure with a destabilizing force. When the murder of Santiago is taking place, the narrator is resting on her 'apostolic' lap (3). It is highly ironic that such a prostitute and brothel owner has apostolic laps and that her apostolic laps, together with her body, offer people not religious consolation or comfort, but sexual, bodily gratification, which is in stark contrast to the Catholic denial of the body.

Miguel de Cervantes is feminized and becomes a seducer who will never sleep. This literary figure is now rewritten and turned into a marginalized and female character who contests the patriarchal culture. The feminized Cervantes is also a seductive woman, which reveals that writing could be regarded as a form of seduction. This in turn implies that this kind of narrative is feminine by nature. A feminine narrative is not and should not be defined by the existence of a female narrator, but it unfolds itself through an act of seduction, like the one in *The Arabian Nights*. *The Arabian Nights* is a case in point in that the stories told in one thousand and one nights are unrolled through the form of narrative seduction so that Scheherazade can defer her death. Through such a kind of narrative seduction, not only King Shahryar's attention, but also the reader's is seduced and captured, so that both her death and the end of reading and narrating will be deferred. As such, the feminine story-telling is not only a form of entertainment, but also a means of death deferment and a way of deferring the end of the narrative. On the other hand, this also means that Scheherazade is the act of reading, and both of her death and the ending of reading are deferred by the continuous unfolding of the seductive text. In this light, reading, (and hence hermeneutics) is a feminine act, revealing a truth which is feminine, which is in line with Nietzsche's view that 'truth is a woman'.[5]

This act of reading is a process drawing the reader to the side of the feminine through the seductive narrative. This seduction of the narrative comes in the form of unending circular movement. The Arabic number '1001' suggests mirror-like repetition and reversal. '10' is mirrored, becomes '01' and then is juxtaposed with its own mirrored image. On another level, the number '1000' represents completeness and totality, but '1001' suggests incompleteness and the necessity to carry on into the next '1000'. In this light, '1001' symbolizes infinity, and this conception of infinity is expressed through the feminine narrative.[6] As such, this is small wonder that the stories told in *The Arabian Nights* come in the form of a labyrinth and a series of interpolating texts, through which unending narrative of seduction is unfolded. This unending thread of narrative is the opposite of Ariadne's thread in

---

5 From 'Preface for the Second Edition' in *The Gay Science* by Friedrich Nietzsche, trans. Walter Kaufmann (New York: Vintage Books, 1974), p. 38, which is discussed in Chapter 4.

6 For more discussion on the idea of infinity, see A.S. Byatt's Introduction to *The Arabian Nights: Tales from A Thousand and One Nights*, trans. Richard F. Burton (New York: The Modern Library, 2001), pp. xiii–xiv.

that it does not lead the reader out of the labyrinth. On the contrary, it draws the reader deeper and deeper into the text.

If María Alejandrina Cervantes represents the seductive power of feminine narrative, which draws the reader into the text through seduction, and if she is the feminized Miguel de Cervantes, it is interesting to question whether Miguel de Cervantes is narrating in a feminine voice in his *Don Quixote*. If narrative is demarcated into two main categories, a masculine one and a feminine one, the former being in the line of Homeric / Hellenistic tradition, while the latter one being in *The Arabian Nights*' line, it is by no means difficult to notice that *Don Quixote* and hence the Hispanic literature fall into the latter category. If so, *Don Quixote* may be written in a 'feminine hand', implying that this masterpiece of the Hispanic literature is a feminine narrative drawing the reader into it through the seduction of a labyrinth of infinite interpolating stories. García Márquez's characters of María Alejandrina Cervantes as a witch-like, seductive and liminal figure and Flora Miguel as a rose of death and curses in this regard raid and destabilize not only Miguel de Cervantes' writing, but also the Hispanic literature, by revealing and exposing their feminine façade which is underplayed, repressed or even concealed in the patriarchal discourse.

The destabilizing force of María Alejandrina Cervantes also manifests itself through her representation of fullness of life and the primacy of the body, which is in stark contrast with the Catholic denial of the body. For most of the time, she is naked:

> I found María Alejandrina Cervantes awake as always at dawn, and completely naked as always when there weren't any strangers in the house. (77)

and the ways she overcomes grief are lovemaking and overeating:

> She was squatting like a Turkish houri on her queenly bed across from a Babylonic platter of things to eat: veal cutlets, a boiled chicken, a pork loin, and a garnishing of plantains and vegetables that would have served five people. Disproportionate eating was always the only way she could mourn and I'd never seen her do it with such grief. I lay down by her side with my clothes on, barely speaking, and mourning too in my way. … I dreamed that a woman was coming into the room with a little girl in her arms, and that the child was chewing without stopping to take a breath and the half-chewed kernels of corn were falling into the woman's brassiere. The woman said to me: "She crunches like a nutty nuthatch, kind of sloppy, kind of slurpy." Suddenly I felt the anxious fingers that were undoing the buttons of my shirt, and I caught the dangerous smell of the beast of love lying by my back, and I felt myself sinking into the delights of the quicksand of her tenderness. But suddenly she stopped, coughed from far off, and slipped out of my life. (77–8)

She mourns in a stately manner – squatting like a Turkish houri on her queenly bed, consuming food enough for five people's consumption. The food is served on a 'Babylonic platter'. The word 'Babylon', according to *OED*, comes from the word 'Babel', which means confusion, especially of language. It refers to the mystical Babylon of the Apocalypse and also means a magnificent abode and a place or city of excessive luxury and wickedness. Hence, the word 'Babylonic' gives a sense of sinfulness, wickedness, excessive luxury and decadence. In this light, this 'Babylonic platter' of food that María Alejandrina Cervantes consumes in order to express her mourning reveals the excessive luxury and magnificence, as well as the decadence and sinfulness not only of her food, her bed and her room, but of her life and her own self as well. Her association with eating is so strong that even in the narrator's dream, she is displaced as a child chewing without stopping. The difference is in reality, she is a woman eating a 'Babylonic platter' of food, but in the dream, she is a child chewing kernels, which is a reversed picture of her waking life. While eating, she attempts to seduce the narrator into lovemaking. Here, she is like the mysterious Moorish woman offering a love potion in a Toledan quince to the Glass Graduate (Cervantes' *Exemplary Stories*, 1998, 112–13). But she stops doing so only when she finds that he smells of Santiago Nasar. It is through disproportionate eating and lovemaking that her mourning is manifested. To her, mourning is in the realm of the sexual. She in this regard symbolizes a propensity towards the body.

7.2. Grotesque Body of Cervantes

But María Alejandrina Cervantes' body is in effect a grotesque body. Bakhtin, in *Rabelais and His World* (1984), associates a grotesque body with hyperboles of food:

> ... one of the oldest forms of hyperbolic grotesque was the exaggerated size of foodstuffs. In this exaggerated form of valuable matter we see for the first time the positive and absolute meaning of size and quantity in an aesthetic image. Hyperboles of food parallel the most ancient hyperboles of belly, mouth, and phallus. (184)

This grotesque exaggeration of the size and the quantity of food is mirrored by María Alejandrina Cervantes' 'disproportionate eating' and her 'Babylonic platter' of food. The image of her consumption of this excessive quantity of food is positive and aesthetic, as this takes place on her 'queenly bed' on which she squats like a Turkish houri.

Another characteristic of a grotesque body, besides disproportionate eating and hyperbolic foodstuffs, is degradation. According to Bakhtin,

> [d]egradation here means coming down to earth, the contact with earth as an element that swallows up and gives birth at the same time. To degrade is to bury, to sow, and to kill simultaneously, in order to bring forth something more and better. To degrade also means to concern oneself with the lower stratum of the body, the life of the belly and the reproductive organs; it therefore relates to acts of defecation and copulation, conception, pregnancy, and birth. Degradation digs a bodily grave for a new birth; it has not only a destructive, negative aspect, but also a regenerating one. To degrade an object does not imply merely hurling

> it into the void of nonexistence, into absolute destruction, but to hurl it down to the reproductive lower stratum, the zone in which conception and a new birth take place. Grotesque realism knows no other lower level; it is the fruitful earth and the womb. It is always conceiving. (*Rabelais and His World*, 1984, 21)

María Alejandrina Cervantes, being a prostitute, is without doubt an obvious figure of degradation. But her body is used as a means of regeneration and her apostolic laps are the source of men's sensual and bodily consolation. She is 'the most elegant and the most tender woman' and above all, 'the most serviceable in bed' (*Chronicle of a Death Foretold*, 65), which implies her skills in copulation. Her bodily seduction, together with her 'illusory calls', ignites Santiago Nasar's 'mad passion' (65) and sparks off a stormy relationship with him, which drives him crazy for 14 months (91). In this regard, her body is metaphorically a 'bodily grave for a new birth'. This new birth, which is also a rebirth experienced through bodily gratification and sensual comfort, raids and destabilizes not only the Catholic ideology of the denial of the body and bodily enjoyment, but also the patriarchal assertion of male supremacy.

This destabilizing rebirth from the body of María Alejandrina Cervantes is a power of creativity and a sense of continual growth, which is another characteristic of the grotesque body.[7] It is Bakhtin's view that,

> the grotesque body … is a body in the act of becoming. It is never finished, never completed; it is continually built, created, and builds and creates another body. Moreover, the body swallows the world and is itself swallowed by the world. … This is why the essential role belongs to those parts of the grotesque body in which it outgrows its own self, transgressing its own body, in which it conceives a new, second body: the bowels and the phallus. …. Next to the bowels and the genital organs is the mouth, through which enters the world to be swallowed up. And next is the anus. … This is why the main events in the life of the grotesque body, the acts of the bodily drama, take place in this sphere. Eating, drinking, defecation and other elimination (sweating, blowing of the nose, sneezing), as well as copulation, pregnancy, dismemberment, swallowing up by another body – all these acts are performed on the confines of the body and the outer world, or on the confines of the old and new body. In all these events the beginning and end of life are closely linked and interwoven. (*Rabelais and His World*, 1984, 317) (original bracketing)

What is of paramount importance is the body and this grotesque body outgrows and outdoes itself by staging a bodily drama of continual becoming. In this sense, the grotesque body is unfinished and incomplete, which is 'based on the conception of the world as eternally unfinished: a world dying and being born at the same time' (166). It also foregrounds creativity as not only is it continually

---

[7] Arnold M. Penuel in *Intertextuality in García Márquez* (Rock Hill, SC: Spanish Literature Publications Company, 1994), especially Chapter 4. 'Carnivalized Discourse in *Cien años de soledad* and *Crónica de una muerte anunciada*' gives a detailed analysis of the grotesque realism of discourse and carnivalisation in this novella.

built and created, it also builds and creates another body. This grotesque body outgrows itself and transgresses its own body, staging a bodily drama through eating, drinking, defecation, copulation, dismemberment, swallowing up by another body, etc. Likewise, María Alejandrina Cervantes stages a bodily drama of eating, drinking and copulation, in which her body swallows up the other and at the same time, being swallowed up. When she swallows up her 'Babylonic platter' of food, she is at the same time swallowed by the decadence of her desire for disproportionate eating and mourning. When she swallows up the other in the process of copulation, she is simultaneously swallowed up as her body is turned into an agent of sensual gratification. In this regard, her body is always in the act of becoming, 'never finished, never completed'. She is like a text unfinished and incomplete.

7.3. Before the Archive

Miguel de Cervantes is turned into María Alejandrina Cervantes, whose grotesque body raids and destabilizes the ideological convention and patriarchal institution by overturning the social and cultural hierarchies. A prostitute eats and lives in a magnificent way like a queen, and influences and dominates others in a witch-like manner. The bodily drama she stages in this regard is carnivalesque, in which hierarchies are undone, raided and subverted, authority loosened and mocked and opposites mingled and abolished. The sacred is profaned, and fantasy becomes fact (Bakhtin's *Problems of Dostoevsky's Poetics*, 1984, 122–6). It is a world turned upside down, inside out. Each and every carnival participant is both actor and spectator, as Bakhtin says,

> Carnival is a pageant without footlights and without a division into performers and spectators. In carnival everyone is an active participant, everyone communes in the carnival act. Carnival is not contemplated and, strictly speaking, not even performed; its participants *live* in it, they live by its laws as long as those laws are in effect; that is, they live a *carnivalistic life*. Because carnivalistic life is life drawn out of its *usual* rut, it is to some extent "life turned inside out," "the reverse side of the world". (*Problems of Dostoevsky's Poetics*, 1984, 122) (original italics)

And hence this is 'a spectacle but without a stage' (Kristeva 1980, 78). In the carnival, there is 'a mighty life-creating and transforming power, an indestructible vitality' and out of which an atmosphere of 'joyful relativity' is generated (Kristeva 1980, 107).

Octavio Paz's idea of the fiesta in essence is analogous to Bakhtin's idea of the carnival. In Paz's view, a fiesta is the undoing of order, the bringing about of a renascence of life and an affirmation of creative energy:

> In certain fiestas the very notion of order disappears. Chaos comes back and license rules. Anything is permitted: the customary hierarchies vanish, along with all social, sex, caste, and trade distinctions. Men disguise themselves as

> women, gentlemen as slaves, the poor as the rich. The army, the clergy, and the law are ridiculed. Obligatory sacrilege, ritual profanation is committed. Love becomes promiscuity. Sometimes the fiesta becomes a Black Mass. Regulations, habits and customs are violated. Respectable people put away the dignified expressions and conservative clothes that isolate them, dress up in gaudy colors, hide behind a mask, and escape from themselves. (Paz 1985, 51)

In a fiesta, order disappears and chaos returns so that social, sex, caste and trade distinctions and hierarchies no longer exist. People are in disguise and become their own opposites. Conventional practices and social norms are no longer valid and authority is ridiculed. But this chaos is constructive and creative in nature:

> The fiesta is a cosmic experiment, an experiment in disorder, reuniting contradictory elements and principles in order to bring about a renascence of life. Ritual death promotes a rebirth; vomiting increases the appetite; the orgy, sterile in itself, renews the fertility of the mother or of the earth. The fiesta is a return to a remote and undifferentiated state, prenatal or presocial. It is a return that is also a beginning, in accordance with the dialectic that is inherent in social processes. (Paz 1985, 51–2)

In this fiesta celebrating a world of chaos, nasty and unpleasant acts become positive and constructive. Opposite elements are united to foster a renascence of life and ritual death will promote a rebirth. Vomiting can help stimulate appetite and the orgy can renew the fertility of the earth. This is a world turned upside down, but this upside down world is a better and more preferable one, especially with regard to creativity:

> … To express it in another way, the fiesta denies society as an organic system of differentiated forms and principles, but affirms it as a source of creative energy. It is a true "re-creation," the opposite of the "recreation" characterizing modern vacations, which do not entail any rites or ceremonies whatever and are as individualistic and sterile as the world that invented them. (Paz 1985, 52)

In other words, a fiesta is a creative energy and a rebirth, which can raid, destabilize and shatter the rigid social hierarchies, forms and principles, out of which a true re-creation is attained. In this light, María Alejandrina Cervantes' 'illusory calls' are in effect carnivalesque laughter, which is a positive and constructive force. Bakhtin states that:

> True ambivalent and universal laughter does not deny seriousness but purifies and completes it. Laughter purifies from dogmatism, from the intolerant and the petrified; it liberates from fanaticism and pedantry, from fear and intimidation, from didacticism, naïveté and illusion, from the single meaning, the single level, from sentimentality. Laughter does not permit seriousness to atrophy and to be torn away from the one being, forever incomplete. It restores this ambivalent wholeness. (*Rabelais and His World*, 1984, 122–3)

This ambivalent laughter is purifying, liberating and restorative. It purifies dogmatism and petrification. It liberates didacticism and intimidation, and undoes single meaning and monolithic interpretation. It restores an undifferentiated pre-natal or pre-social state. María Alejandrina Cervantes thus is a Siren turned positive. Instead of capturing and killing the other, she is liberating and invigorating.

In this light, there is a carnivalising labyrinth in this novella. This is a destabilizing and feminizing labyrinth housed not a masculine Minotaur, but an emasculated one. In this labyrinth, there is a carnivalesque murder in which everybody in the village is both the spectator and the actor in the grotesque bodily drama of murdering Santiago Nasar. There are numerous festive occasions and comical mischances which lead to a senseless murder staged as a public spectacle in the main square of the town. It is only in such a carnival that this 'senseless' murder becomes legitimate. Various attempts are made to stop the crime and to let Santiago Nasar know about the coming of the Vicario brothers to kill him, but all these attempts, whether verbal or written, are in vain mysteriously. Flora Miguel, the fiancée of Santiago Nasar, could have warned him about this and so prevented the crime and saved his life, but her feelings of humiliation and rage get the better of her, which turns a warning to a curse and a death wish. Likewise, written warnings or letters are also futile:

> Someone who was never identified had shoved an envelope under the door with a piece of paper warning Santiago Nasar that they were waiting for him to kill him, and, in addition, the note revealed the place, the motive, and other quite precise details of the plot. The message was on the floor when Santiago Nasar left home but he didn't see it, nor did Divina Flor or anyone else until long after the crime had been consummated. (12–13)

This anonymous paper is as mysterious as the way the murder of Santiago Nasar is committed. What is significant is not the source, the origin, or the author of this piece of forgotten paper, but the fact that it is there but unseen before the crime. It seems uncannily invisible lying on the floor, which escapes the notice of its intended recipient, or of Divina Flor, or of others.[8] This can be likened to the situation in Poe's 'The Purloined Letter'. On the one hand, this reveals the dysfunctioning of language, and especially in García Márquez's novella, the failure and the inadequacy of both writing and speech for the purposes and functions they are intended. On the other hand, writing now conceals itself in its revelation and exposure. This can also be found in Borges' 'The Garden of Forking Paths', in which the secret of the whereabouts of the British artillery park is concealed by being revealed in a newspaper. The mysterious paper in *Chronicle of a Death Foretold* not only escapes the attention of its intended recipient (that is, Nasar), but also represents a message deferred. This is a message which will not arrive at its destination, and has to be read afterward, after the crime. It is a special kind of posthumous paper, read not after the death of the author, but after the death of its recipient, like Derrida's 'shopping list'.[9]

---

[8] For the discussion on this mysterious piece of paper, see Isabel Alvarez-Borland's 'From Mystery to Parody: (Re)Readings of García Márquez's *Cronica de una muerte anunciada*' in *Garbriel García Márquez* ed. Harold Bloom, pp. 223–4.

[9] Discussed in Chapter 5.

The murder of Santiago Nasar becomes a carnivalesque spectacle, but this spectacle is not without cruelty. Not only is the act of murder violent, but the way the autopsy is conducted also shows how cruelly and badly Santiago Nasar's body is mutilated and re-mutilated:

> The priest [Father Carmen Amador] had studied medicine and surgery at Salamanca, but had entered the seminary before he was graduated, and even the mayor knew that his autopsy would have no legal standing. Nevertheless, he made him carry out the order.
>
> It was a massacre, performed at the public school with the help of the druggist, who took notes, and a first-year medical student who was here on vacation. … Seven of the several wounds were fatal. The liver was almost sliced in pieces by two deep cuts on the anterior side. He had four incisions in the stomach, one of them so deep that it went completely through and destroyed the pancreas. He had six other lesser perforations in the transverse colon and multiple wounds in the small intestine. … (74–5)

and such a description of the mutilation afflicted upon Santiago Nasar's body and of the autopsy ironically regarded as another 'massacre' goes on for nearly two pages. At the beginning of this autopsy section of the novella (Section 4), Father Carmen Amador is presented as a substitute, a supplement:

> The damage from the knives was only a beginning for the inclement autopsy that Father Carmen Amador found himself obliged to do in Dr Dionisio Iguarán's absence. "It was as if we killed him all over again after he was dead," the aged priest told me in his retirement at Calafell. (72)

Dr. Dionisio Iguarán is an allusion to the Greek god Dionysus while Father Amador, whose name means 'lover', is having a female first name 'Carmen', which carnivalises his gender and implies that this Father is a girl lover. Now Dionysus is absent and Father Carmen Amador substitutes his place to conduct the autopsy. First, this implies that the supplementation of a Dionysian drive for orgiastic celebration of life by a religious force will only result in massacre and destruction.[10] This destruction is inflicted not only upon the living, but upon the

---

[10] A similar argument is made in 'Fathers and Virgins: García Márquez's Faulknerian *Chronicle of a Death Foretold*' by John S. Christie, in *Latin American Literary Review*, Volume XXI, Number 41 (January-June 1993), pp. 21–9. On p. 25, it reads 'Symbolically, Father Amador becomes the medical examiner in place of Dionisio – religious authority being closer to death than is Dionysian distinct.' Also see Arnold Penuel's 'The Sleep of Vital Reason in García Márquez's *Cronica de una muerte anunciada'* in *Critical Essays on Gabriel García Márquez*, ed. George R. McMurray, p. 197. For a different view regarding Derrida's idea of supplement in relation to this text, see Carlos Alonso's 'Writing and ritual in *Chronicle of a Death Foretold*' in *Gabriel García Márquez: New Readings* ed. Bernard McGuirk and Richard Cardwell (Cambridge: Cambridge University Press, 1987), in which Nasar's entrails are regarded as 'a surplus, a supplement that must be discarded' (p. 162).

already dead as well, as Father Amador admits that the whole autopsy is so brutally done that it seems he and his assistants have killed Santiago Nasar all over again after he is dead. In other words, this supplement is a kind of killing, bringing death to both the living and the dead. Like Shakespeare's Juliet who has to die twice, once before and once after Romeo's death,[11] Santiago Nasar fares in a similar way. But the difference is, when Santiago Nasar dies twice, the first time is real and the second time is metaphorical, while in Juliet's case, the first time is fake and the second time is real. Because of this death after death, rather than resurrection after death, it is small wonder that they return 'a completely different body' of Santiago Nasar to his family after this 'religious' autopsy.[12]

This supplement is needed for such a fragmented text. The carving up of the body of Santiago Nasar can be likened to the cutting up of a text, resulting in the absence of the plot. If Nasar's body is viewed as an archive, after his body is cut up by the twin brothers Pedro and Pablo and after it is raided and dismembered in this autopsy, this archive no longer exists. As this bodily text is dismembered and the manuscripts are fragmented, the archive falls into pieces. Because of the loss and disappearance of the archive, a supplement is necessary, resulting in endless and fruitless accumulation of fragmented details, memories and manuscripts for the crime, supplementing each other only to defer the meaning of the murder.

Second, the whole autopsy is now veiled with a religious undertone and hence the autopsy report says 'It looked like a stigma of the crucified Christ' (76).[13] The name 'Nasar' is an obvious allusion to Christ, as it is in the Bible:

> And he came and dwelt in a city called Nazareth, that it might be fulfilled which was spoken by the prophets, "He shall be called a Nazarene." (Matthew, 2:23, King James version)

But this 'crucified Christ' will not enjoy any resurrection after his death, but a death after death, a repetition of death. Third, this also shows a carnivalesque mixture of heterogeneous elements: a crime investigation through a religious rite in a setting of a medical autopsy. This autopsy in effect is more like a carnival than a religious ceremony or a medical or crime investigation.

---

[11] Discussed by Jacques Derrida in 'Aphorism Countertime' in *Acts of Literature* ed. Derek Attridge (New York and London: Routledge, 1992), p. 422.

[12] For the idea of ritual repetition of the murder of Santiago Nasar enacted through the narrative, see Carlos Alonso's 'Writing and ritual in *Chronicle of a Death Foretold*' in *Gabriel García Márquez: New Readings*, ed. Bernard McGuirk and Richard Cardwell, especially pp. 156–60, in which Nasar's autopsy is regarded as 'a murder beyond murder' (p. 160). For Nasar's double death, see 'From Mystery to Parody: (Re)Readings of García Márquez's *Cronica de nua muerte anunciada*' by Isabel Alvarez-Borland, in *Gabriel García Márquez*, ed. Harold Bloom (New York: Chelsea House Publisher, 1989), pp. 225–6.

[13] For Nasar is the figure of Christ, see Arnold Penuel's 'The Sleep of Vital Reason in García Márquez's *Cronica de una muerte anunciada*' in *Critical Essays on Gabriel García Márquez*, ed. George R. McMurray, pp. 197 and 202.

The carnival implicit in this novella is of a violent nature. This goes in line with Nietzsche's idea that

> Without cruelty there is no festival: thus the longest and most ancient part of human history teaches – and in punishment there is so much that is *festive*![14] (original italics)

and Octavio Paz thinks alike:

> The art of the fiesta has been debased almost everywhere else, but not in Mexico. There are few places in the world where it is possible to take part in a spectacle like our great religious fiestas with their *violent* primary colors, their bizarre costumes and dances, their fireworks and ceremonies, and their inexhaustible welter of surprises: the fruit, candy, toys and other objects sold on these days in the plazas and open-air markets. (1985, 47) (italics added)

It seems that the carnival and the fiesta are equivalent. At the core of the carnival is a primary colour of violence without which it will not come into being. On the surface, this novella can be viewed as a critique of the cults of virginity and honour, because of which, the Vicario brothers justify their murder of Santiago Nasar even though it is done in front of the villagers. On another level, this novella is a mockery of the Catholic denial of the body and its inadequacy when it deals with issues which involves dominant social cults. At the heart of these focuses is a carnivalesque drive propelling the momentum of not only the actions of the characters, but also the progression of this feminine narrative. If so, the whole novella can be viewed in this way: at the core of this act of violence is a carnival, which is framed and coated by a religious mockery, which then is framed and coated by a cultural critique of the cults of virginity and honour. If the novella is read in this way, what underpins the violent murder of Santiago Nasar, the mockery of Catholicism and the critique of outmoded cults is a carnival.

This chronicle, which aims to record and retell the facts of the murder of Santiago Nasar, is a deceiving one. It is a deceiving manuscript as the carnivalesque nature of the violent crime is now disguised as an act to safeguard the cult of honour. Paradoxically, this manuscript is housed in a patriarchal archive:

> Twelve days after the crime, the investigating magistrate came upon a town that was an open wound. … He was newly graduated and still wore his black linen law school suit and the gold ring with the emblem of his degree, and he had the airs and the lyricism of a happy new parent. But I never learned his name. Everything we know about his character has been learned from the brief, which several people helped me look for twenty years later in the Palace of Justice in Riohacha. There was no classification of files whatever and more than a century of cases were piled up on the floor of the decrepit colonial building that had been Sir Francis Drake's headquarters for two days. The ground floor would

---

[14] From the Second Essay, Section 6 of *On the Genealogy of Morals* by Friedrich Nietzsche, trans. Walter Kaufmann (New York: Vintage Books, 1989), p. 67.

> be flooded by high tides and the unbound volumes floated about the deserted offices. I myself did my searching many times with the water up to my ankles in that lagoon of lost causes, and only chance after five years of searching let me rescue some 322 pages filched from the more than 500 that the brief must have had. (99–100)

This archive is situated in 'a decrepit colonial building that had been Sir Francis Drake's headquarters' now named as 'the Palace of Justice in Riohacha'. There is an obvious connection among the archive, colonialism and the carnival. In this archive, instead of one authoritative archon, there are several destabilizing voices. The first one is Sir Francis Drake, who is said to have employed this building as his headquarters for two days. Sir Francis Drake is a famous English naval hero, who was the vice admiral of the fleet that destroyed the Spanish Armada in 1588. In 1587, with a fleet of some 30 ships, he stormed into the Spanish harbour of Cadiz and in 36 hours destroyed thousands of tons of shipping and supplies destined for the Armada. In 1588, he used fire ships to drive the Armada out of Calais, where it had taken refuge, and as a result, the Spanish fleet was dispersed and largely wrecked. Sir Francis Drake is also a well-known explorer who was the first Englishman to circumnavigate the world in the sixteenth century.[15] He is a symbol of the Age of Voyage and Discovery and the spirit of exploration. But exploration often goes hand in hand with exploitation and one of the many aspects of the Age of Voyage may be a disguise of colonialism. By mentioning that the decrepit colonial building was once the headquarters of Sir Francis Drake, which means it is in fact his archive,[16] colonialism is now implicitly twisted and turned to be a critique of itself. Latin America had been subjected to Spanish colonial invasion and domination since the fifteenth century,[17] so Spain to Latin America was a huge colonial force. But here Sir Francis Drake represents another colonial force undoing the Spanish one. If so, this archive can be regarded as a mockery and a reminder of the decline of Spanish colonialism, which went hand in hand with the decline of Spain.

Now this dilapidated archive is deserted, representing the presence of law as origin of the narrative being hollowed out. The power of this archive in a word is suspended. What is left is incomplete documents and fragmented manuscripts floating in water.[18]

---

[15] Factual details concerning Sir Francis Drake are from "Sir Francis Drake" *Encyclopædia Britannica* from Encyclopædia Britannica Online. http://search.eb.com/eb/article?eu=31649.

[16] Derrida points out that 'archive' etymologically refers to 'the residence of the superior magistrates, the archons' in *Archive Fever* p. 2. See also González Echevarría's *Myth and archive* p. 31.

[17] "Latin America" *Encyclopædia Britannica* from Encyclopædia Britannica Online. http://search.eb.com/eb/article?eu=48395.

[18] For more discussion along this line, see González Echevarría's *Myth and Archive*, pp. 177–9.

The second destabilizing voice of this archive is the unnamed judge. This nameless judge is a newly graduate from a law school, still wearing 'his black linen law school suit and the gold ring with emblem of his degree' (99). It seems that he is Tomás Rodaja before becoming the Glass Graduate. He is also a man with a feverish passion for literature:

> The judge's name didn't appear on any of them, but it was obvious that he was a man burning with the fever of literature. He had doubtless read the Spanish classics and a few Latin ones, and he was quite familiar with Nietzsche, who was the fashionable author among magistrates of his time. The marginal notes, and not just because of the color of the ink, seemed to be written in blood. He was so perplexed by the enigma that chance had touched him with, that many times he fell into lyrical distractions that ran contrary to the rigor of his profession. Most of all, he never thought it legitimate that life should make use of so many coincidences forbidden literature, so that there should be the untrammeled fulfillment of a death so clearly foretold. (100)

As he is 'burning with the fever of literature', a person with an *archive fever* for literature, he must be well acquainted with the Spanish classics, and without doubt, he must have read Cervantes' *Don Quixote*. The link between this nameless judge and Don Quixote may lie in the quest for their impossible dream. When this investigating magistrate still wet behind the ears is baffled by the crime, very often he falls into lyrical distractions contrary to his profession, which requires a rational mind for constructing causality out of fragmented past events. It is his quixotic quest to unravel the enigma that 'life should make use of so many coincidences forbidden literature'. The crime that he has to investigate is full of 'coincidences' which are forbidden to literature, especially realist literature which is supposed not to stress coincidence or chance. It is intriguing to him that what is in front of him is a real life abounding with coincidences which go beyond the law of literature. This is a real life being fictionalized through coincidences, or a fiction being realized by chance. It is more intriguing that with a blurring or disappearance of the boundary between the real and the fictional, there is an 'untrammeled fulfillment of a death so clearly foretold'. This demolition of the demarcation between the real and the fictional is exactly what is experienced in a carnival, and such 'a death so clearly foretold' refers of course to Santiago Nasar's death. In this sense, Santiago Nasar in fact dies in a carnival full of 'coincidences forbidden literature'. It is obvious that this unnamed judge is not only a figure symbolizing the synthesis of law and literature, the law of literature and the literature of law, but also a person torn between these contrary disciplines.

Besides having a literary passion, he is also familiar with Nietzsche's works. Nietzsche, one of the masters of suspicion, is described as a fashionable author among magistrates at that time. It is ironic that a judge pronouncing authoritative unambiguous verdicts will be interested in a philosopher of nihilism. It may be that by being interested in Nietzsche, the judge shows himself as an avant-garde person. But the real reason for this is never certain. To this unnamed judge, what is feverishly burning within himself is literature, his passion and fever for manuscripts. It is this feverish literature that burns the archive, resulting in a case of murder full of 'coincidences forbidden literature'. Hence, he is unable to construct a plot for this murder foretold, for this chronicle of a Nasar's death foretold.

But he is not the real judge. The real judge seems to be Angela Vicario, who names Santiago Nasar and thus pronounces a judicial sentence.[19] She is a peculiar judge not in the sense that the gender of this judge is now feminine, as the issue of gender has already been made problematic in the novella. She is a peculiar judge in the sense that by naming Santiago Nasar as the perpetrator ('He was my perpetrator.') (101), she is doing two things at once: sentencing Santiago to death as the code of honour is set in motion by her words, and proclaiming that she is the victim. But it is worth noting that she is forced to name a perpetrator under the patriarchal pressure. She is actually a prisoner of patriarchy rather than a judge. It is never sure and it is in fact never possible to figure out who is the real judge. Or the fact is it is impossible to have a real judge for this murder foretold.

Another destabilizing voice in this flooded colonial archive, in a metaphorical sense, comes from the narrator. In compiling their unambiguously ambiguous chronicle, he not only has to gather documents and manuscripts from this archive and interview numerous witnesses, but he also has to resort to his own memory, no matter how faulty it is. In this light, his memory, although not as absolute as Funes' or not as formidable as the Glass Graduate's, is a supplement to the chronicle in that, it makes up for what the chronicle is missing and at the same time, it is something extra, surplus. Having these three sources of information in front of him, the narrator is like an investigative reporter who returns to 'this forgotten village, trying to put the broken mirror of memory back together from so many scattered shards' (5).[20] The manuscripts and memories that the narrator has are like 'scattered shards' out of which he wishes to construct a totality. It is like he tries to piece together the fragmented body of Santiago Nasar in order to get a glimpse of what he looks like before his murder. If Nasar's body is likened to an archive, this is an archive in pieces. It is an archive which is unable to offer a complete whole. What it can offer are fragmented bodies of manuscripts and memories. Because of the absence of a complete whole, the text fails to offer a plot of the crime, in which the narrator's attempts to construct causality of the events are always in vain.

Instead of a single authoritative archon, there are plural voices revealing not only a babelization of voices, but also the impossibility of the archive. Because of this, this chronicle has got too many 'authoritative' voices that at the end no authority or meaning can be stabilized. It is a carnival full of authoritative voices,

---

[19] Detailed discussion about Angela Vicario's decisive roles in the novella can be found in Gonzalo Diaz-Migoyo's 'Truth Disguised: *Chronicle of a Death* (Ambiguously) *Foretold*' in *Gabriel García Márquez and the Powers of Fiction*, ed. Julio Ortega (Austin: University of Texas Press, 1988), pp. 74–86 and John S. Christie's 'Fathers and Virgins: García Márquez's Faulknerian *Chronicle of a Death Foretold*' in *Latin American Literary Review*, Volume XXI, Number 41, pp. 21–9.

[20] This is discussed by Elena M. de Costa when reviewing this novella in *Latin American Literary Review*, Volume XI, Fall–Winter 1982, Number 21, pp. 63–7 (Pittsburgh: University of Pittsburgh).

hence making itself de-authoritative. Likewise, the whole village is full of such voices that Santiago Nasar cannot help feeling baffled:

> They began to shout at him from every side, and Santiago Nasar went backward and forward several times, baffled by so many voices at the same time. It was obvious that he was heading toward his house through the kitchen door, but suddenly he must have realized that the main door was open. … "At first he was startled," Clotilde Armenta told me, "because he didn't know who was shouting at him or from where." But when he saw her he also saw Pedro Vicario, who threw her to the ground and caught up with his brother. Santiago Nasar was less than fifty yards from his house and he ran to the main door. (117–18)

Santiago is not sure from whom or from where the voice comes and inevitably loses his bearings and rationality in such a labyrinth of voices.

Besides the presence of multiple authoritative voices and hence of none, this is also an archive by which it is implied that chaos and disorder are preferred. Classification of files is not possible. This deserted archive has been flooded for such a long time that it is actually a 'lagoon of lost causes'. Causes are lost in the fluidity of water, rationality cannot be relied upon and causality cannot be established. Contrary to Eco's archive in *The Name of the Rose*, which is raided and destroyed by fire, this colonial archive of García Márquez's is raided and decomposed by flood. Only 322 pages out of more than 500 are rescued from water after the narrator's five-year search. But how does he know there should be more than 500 pages when he only recovers 322? There may be only 323 pages, added with the anonymous piece of the forgotten paper that escapes Santiago Nasar's and others' attention on the day of his being murdered, or there may be 1,001 pages, most of which have been washed away by high tides to the Caribbean. It seems that the part cannot establish the whole in this 'lagoon of lost causes' in this apocalyptic flood, which raids, devours and destroys not only the manuscripts, but also the archive.

This is also foretold by Wordsworth in *The Prelude.*[21] As discussed in Chapter 1 that the shell in the narrator's Arabian dream stands for an apocalyptic call, an apocalyptic warning and an end-of-the-world reminder. It is ironic that such apocalyptic destruction by deluge manifests itself through 'a loud prophetic blast of harmony', encased in a beautiful dazzling shell. Wordsworth's apocalyptic flood comes in the form of 'a bed of glittering light' and in no time, 'the waters of the deep' gather upon the narrator and the mysterious Arab, who is the double of Don Quixote, has to hurry over the 'illimitable waste' because 'the fleet waters of a drowning world' is pouring towards him in order to engulf and destroy him.

In *Chronicle of a Death Foretold*, this apocalyptic flood does not come in the form of harmony encased in a shell, but in the chaos of a 'decrepit colonial building', where 'a century of cases are piled up here and there on the floor, and soaked manuscripts and 'unbound volumes' are floating about the deserted offices on the ground floor. This apocalyptic flood itself is the destruction of the archive, a site where records of the crime is kept, but this destruction does not arouse any

---

[21] *The Prelude, 1799, 1805, 1850*, the 1850 edition, Book 5, ll. 88–99 and ll. 125–40.

terror. Instead, this significantly reveals the irrelevance of the archive to people's lives. At the same time, it creates a scene of an archive turned upside down through an apocalyptic flood.

As González Echevarría points out, water in this dilapidated archive turns the floor into a mirror, which reflects but cannot support anything. This is 'an inverted law overarching yet undermining the constitution of the text'. Moreover, the manuscripts floating in the water are directly opposite to those which are solidly grounded. This implies the collapse of stable symbolic meanings (González Echevarría 1998, 179). Gone with the archons is the authority of these manuscripts in this deserted archive.

Because of this apocalyptic flood, this decrepit colonial archive is turned into a solitary labyrinth, with deserted offices and incomplete manuscripts dissolved by water for years. This becomes an archive of solitude soaked with a sense of emptiness. Octavio Paz says that 'solitude and orphanhood are similar forms of emptiness' (Paz 1985, 207), because of alienation:

> Solitude – the feeling and knowledge that one is alone, alienated from the world and oneself – is not an exclusively Mexican characteristic. All men, at some moment in their lives, feel themselves to be alone. … Man is the only being who knows he is alone, and the only one who seeks out another. His nature … consists in his longing to realize himself in another. Man is nostalgia and a search for communion. Therefore, when he is aware of himself he is aware of his lack of another, that is, of his solitude. (Paz 1985, 195)

Solitude makes you feel you yourself are alone, and it is a sense of alienation, not only from the world, but also from yourself. Out of this sense of aloneness and alienation, you long for realizing yourself in another. As you are aware of your lack and your emptiness, you are aware of your solitude and thus are in search of communion. This sense of alienating emptiness, original lack and primal loss comes into being when the tie between us and the maternal womb is severed:

> When we are born we break the ties that joined us to the blind life we lived in the maternal womb, where there is no gap between desire and satisfaction. We sense the change as separation and loss, as abandonment, as a fall in a strange or hostile atmosphere. Later this primitive sense of loss becomes a feeling of solitude, and still later it becomes awareness: we are condemned to live alone, but also to transcend our solitude, to re-establish the bonds that united us with life in a paradisiac past. All our forces strive to abolish our solitude. (Paz 1985, 195)

In order to transcend or abolish our solitude, it is necessary to re-establish communion which unites us not only with the other, be it a human, an object or the world, but also with 'life in a paradisiac past' before the break between us and our maternal womb or life. A child restores this by means of play and affection and 'thanks to games and fantasies, the inert natural world of adults – a chair, a book, anything – suddenly acquires a life of its own.' This reveals the dual significance of solitude – a break with one world and an attempt to create another (Paz 1985, 202–4).

7.4. Solitude and Utopia

The archive of solitude breaks away from the realistic world and at the same time, creates another world of its own by dismantling and destabilizing hierarchies and genders, mocking and multiplying authorities, and shaking and subverting the demarcation between fiction and real life. Like a child who breaks free the world of adults and creates his own world through games and fantasies and through play and affection, this carnivalising archive does likewise by what Bakhtin calls a 'mighty life-creating and transforming power, an indestructible vitality' (*Problems of Dostoevsky's Poetics*, 1984, 107), by hyperboles and promiscuity foregrounded, and by violence and authority ridiculed, and by carnivalisation and grotesque realism invigorated in a context of an archive of a carnival.

According to Octavio Paz, another characteristic of solitude is that it is a fiesta in which the chronometric time is destroyed and the eternal present is reinstated. As the feeling of solitude is a nostalgic longing for the body from which man was cast out, it is also a longing for a place, which is 'the centre of the world, the navel of the universe'. Man has thus been expelled from the centre of the world and from eternity. Since this exile, he has become a prisoner of the chronometric time:

> When man was exiled from that eternity in which all times were one, he entered chronometric time and became a prisoner of the clock and the calendar. As soon as time was divided up into yesterday, today and tomorrow, into hours, minutes and seconds, man ceased to be one with time, ceased to coincide with the flow of reality. (Paz 1985, 209)

The loss of eternity forces man to fall into the chronometric time and to become its prisoner, and time and reality since then have been separated. However, this imprisoning time can be liberated and eternity can be regained only in the mythological time of myths and fiestas:

> Mythological time … is impregnated with all the particulars of our lives: it is as long as eternity or as short as a breath, ominous or propitious, fecund or sterile. This idea allows for the existence of a number of varying times. Life and time coalesce to form a single whole, an indivisible unity. … A fiesta is more than a date or anniversary. It does not celebrate an event: it *reproduces* it. Chronometric time is destroyed and the eternal present – for a brief but immeasurable period – is reinstated. The fiesta becomes the creator of time; repetition becomes conception. (Paz 1985, 209–10) (original italics)

This mythological time can be found not only in myths, but also in carnivals, in both of which time is re-created so that life and time will not be separated. But this has to be achieved by the co-existence of varying, heterogeneous times for life and time to coalesce into an indivisible unity, through which, man can 'emerge from his solitude and become one with creation' (Paz 1985, 211). The original concept of the archive as a homogenizing, totalizing and paralyzing structure is raided, rewritten and transformed by García Márquez into an archive, resisting the chronometric time by allowing the existence of various and varying voices to dominate itself concurrently. Sir Francis Drake is a figure of the sixteenth century. Angela Vicario names Santiago Nasar as the criminal one night before he is murdered. The nameless judge comes 12 days after the murder. The narrator returns to this unnamed village 27 years after Santiago's murder to judge the validity of each and every bit of manuscripts and memories shattered like mirror shards. This carnivalising archive is actually a labyrinth of voices raiding and destabilizing not only meaning but also authority.

But what kind of mythological time does this archive create? What kind of 'a single whole, an indivisible unity' does the mythological time of this carnival bring forth? As discussed in Chapter 1, in Melquíades' archive in *One Hundred Years of Solitude*, its mythological time not only resists the circular time outside it (210, 356 and 361), but also stabilizes an eternal Monday and an eternal March and thus resists changes and contamination. As such, it is a 'small isolated room where the arid air never penetrated, nor the dust, nor the heat' (375), and a room 'immune to dust and destruction' (280). A wholeness is achieved, the signifier and the signified are reunited and the meaning of the Buendía's history is made meaningful and intelligible when Melquíades' Sanskrit manuscript is deciphered, which also coincides with the close of the novel and the end of 100 years of solitude. This utopian unity is like the one described in Cervantes' 'The Dialogue of the Dogs', in which Berganza dreams of resuming his proper guise. However, in the archive in *Chronicle of a Death Foretold*, the mythological time foregrounds a labyrinth of heterogeneous voices, the impossibility of piecing together parts to form a totality, the oblivion of totality because parts are continuously dissolving, and a rebirth and a celebration of chaos and disorder effected by a carnival. The chronometric time is destroyed, but eternity is nowhere in sight. If there is an eternity, this will only be an eternity of chaos and disunity. In this light, the archive seems to be a place of eternal chaos.

The archive in *Chronicle of a Death Foretold* is like an empty signifier, a fabula without a sjuzet. It tries to give a narrative, but is unable to do so. There is the absence and the impossibility of a plot within the archive, in which manuscripts are floating in water, shattered like mirror shards. In other words, this novella is anti-archival, offering only an empty shell of archive in which manuscripts can never be homogenized into a totalizable narrative.

PART 4
Archives Go Soft

Chapter 8
Archives in the Age of Technology

Cervantes plays a very important role with regard to the concepts of the archive and the manuscript. He offers a 'lost' archive through Don Quixote. Don Quixote's library is burned by the priest because it is believed that it is the source and the cause of his madness (Part 1, Chapter 6). Cervantes is not only the 'founder' of this 'lost' archive, which is damned by the priest, the barber and Don Quixote's niece, but a raider of his own archive. Cervantes raids the archive by the presence of a non-originating Toledo manuscript (Part 1, Chapter 9), by displacing realities and appearances through tropelía and by the liberating and utopian discourse of the witch Cañizares. This foregrounds the importance of the feminine seductive text and the liberating female narrator in unsettling the originating and patriarchal centre of the archive. Certainly, Cervantes is aware of the dangers and violence of the archive. Raided by Cervantes, the archive is no longer complete, and totality is only an illusion. It is the victim of burning or fever, or in Wordsworth's re-reading of Don Quixote and in García Márquez's *Chronicle of a Death Foretold*, it is the victim of flooding. The archive is burning in two ways – the burning of the archive as in *Don Quixote*,[1] and the burning inside the archive, as discussed in Derrida's *Archive Fever*.

The writings of Borges, Puig and García Márquez can be regarded as in Cervantes' shadow and as postcolonial responses to his 'lost' archive through raiding. They raid the archive through writing, and in this light, writing comes in the form of raiding. Cervantes' witch Cañizares in 'The Dialogue of the Dogs' and the mysterious Moorish woman in 'The Glass Graduate' are turned by Puig into the feminine narrator Molina, who liberates not only Valentin's mind, but also his sexuality. García Márquez also responds to Cervantes' female witch and seductive women by playfully feminizing Cervantes as the character María Alejandrina Cervantes in *Chronicle of a Death Foretold*, who is not only liberating as Puig's Molina, but also carnivalesque, representing a destabilization of patriarchal authority and hierarchy and a utopian desire for rebirth. In Cervantes, Puig and García Márquez, the primacy of the female narrator, which can be traced from *The Arabian Nights* and Rojas' *Celestina*, suggests that Latin American literature is a literature which urges us to talk *to* the woman, not to talk *about* the woman.

This theme is captured by Pedro Almodóvar's film *Talk to Her* (2002). The film opens with two blind women dancing through a world of obstacles of tables and chairs. This image allegorizes repressive Spain in the 1940s and 50s under the rule of Francisco Franco, who turned Spain into a police state and who was prepared to inhabit a Europe controlled by Hitler (Southworth 2002, 187–91). In the film, this is symbolized through the two women in coma, Alicia (a ballet dancer) and

---

1 Also in Eco's *The Name of the Rose* as discussed in Chapter 5.

Lydia (a female bullfighter), who are spoken to by the two lonely men Benigno (a male nurse) and Marco (a journalist). It seems that they offer themselves as a seductive text, narrative or manuscript for the two male protagonists to respond to, to talk to. It also seems that these two women have a lot to tell, but because of their coma, it is impossible to do so. The same situation happens to Latin America – full of stories to tell, but somehow unable to do so. So it is personified as a woman to talk *to*, but not to talk *about*. Gerald Martin in *Journeys through the Labyrinth* likens the history of Latin America to a case of a rape:

> Mother America, aboriginal, virgin, fertile, creative and productive – nature's muse – was violated by the Spaniard, the European outsider, cold, rationalistic and covetous, motivated by theories, not experience, by lust and power, not love and understanding. The product of this assault was the illegitimate Mestizo (of mixed blood), the Latin American culture hero. Its effect is felt to this day whenever Latin Americans gaze at the spectacle of their history and ponder their identity: for theirs is not an identity but a duality: Indian/Spaniard, female/male, America/Europe, country/city, matter/spirit, barbarism/civilization, nature/culture, and perhaps most ironic in the context of Latin American fiction, speech/writing. (Martin 1989, 11)

Since then, Latin Americans have embarked on a long and solitary journey in a double labyrinth – a European one and an American one. This shows not only the post-colonial hybridity of Latin America, but also the importance of a text narrated by a marginalized feminine narrator.

Like Cervantes' Toledo manuscript, Borges, Puig and García Márquez raid the archive by bringing in a destabilizing, non-originating and non-totalizable manuscript. In Borges's 'The Library of Babel', what is in pursuit is an impossible total book. In Puig's *Kiss of the Spider Woman*, the police archive houses a report on Molina and Valentin, followed a dialogue in which Molina temporarily manipulates the patriarchal agents. At the same time, the archive of the Hollywood 'B' movies is raided by the existence of a fictional film story among the real ones. In the like manner, a fake text is inserted in the archive on homosexuality, which comes in the form of footnotes. In García Márquez's *Chronicle of a Death Foretold*, there is a non-totalizable chronicle in which it is impossible to have a plot for the story.

These three raiders and writers of the archive, of the 'lost' archive, in Cervantes' shadow and together with Cervantes, playfully undo the concept of the archive. They reveal not only the archive's impossibility to tell the truth and to narrate, but also the fictionality of the archive, how facts are fictionalized within the archive, and how fiction makes things up in the archive. They unsettle the archive through 'play'. 'Play' in this context can be understood in two ways. First, these raiders and writers of the lost archive are creatively playful to turn and twist the paralyzed structure of the archive. Cervantes does it through tropelía, which confuses reality and appearance; Borges plays with the possibility and limit of the archive through excessive memories and a limitless library; Puig twists the archive through the seductive narrative of a homosexual unsettling sexuality and authority of patriarchy; and finally, García Márquez turns the archive into a place in which it is impossible to tell a story, to construct a plot out of a story, to locate the signified in the signifier. After it has been playfully raided by these writers, the archive is taken apart, and hence it is no longer totalizing or totalizable.

Second, from Derrida's point of view, in 'Structure, Sign and Play in the Discourse of the Human Sciences', 'play' can be understood as 'the disruption of presence' (Derrida 1978, 292). All structures have a 'centre' which all elements in the structure refer and connect to. This centre is irreplaceable as it makes the structure hold its shape and keep all the parts together. This is the self-sufficiency and absolute completion of the centre, which is grounded in the presence. For anything to be understood in terms of presence to be self-sufficient, what needs to be overlooked is signifying absence. There could be no presence without such absence. But this stability and fixity established by the centre limits the movement of the elements in the structure, to have no play at all, to be stable and become fully present. The movement limited is 'play' and this idea of 'play' works against the ideas of self-sufficiency and absolute completion of the centre. In order to disrupt such presence, 'play is always play of absence and presence' (Derrida 1978, 292) through the movement of supplementarity to show the inconsistencies, instability of such presence or self-sufficiency.

The archive is a totalizing structure whose stability does not allow any movement of play in it. The structurality of the archive, in other words, is the absence of play. But the raiders of the archive deliberately foreground the movement of play, the movement of supplementarity within the archive so that the binary opposites of presence and absence are no longer in place. In the Cave of Montesinos, Don Quixote experiences the collapse of spatial opposites of inside / outside, and temporal opposites of present / past. In Borges's 'Funes the Memorious', the distinction between generality and specificity no longer holds, as in Funes' memories and archive, generalization and abstraction are impossible. Puig problematizes heterosexuality / homosexuality and factuality / fictionality, bringing down not only the archives of police documents and Hollywood B-movies, but also the archival discourse on homosexuality. García Márquez plays with the interplay between the body and its parts, stressing the impossibility of constructing a totality out of its parts. The consistency and self-sufficiency of the archive as a centre are undone through play, and as a result, the whole structure of the archive no longer remains stable.

The essences of the archive are origin and authority, but now these essences are taken away by these raiders and writers of the archive. The power of origin is put in question by the existence of fictional manuscripts, which at the same time destabilizes the authority in terms of authorship and attributability. These postcolonial writers remain in Cervantes' shadow and at the same time are playful with it. They raid Cervantes' archive feverishly. It seems in their response to the colonizing shadow of Cervantes, they are solitary yet utopian, and such characters abound in the works of these raiders. It is no coincidence that the themes of solitude and utopianism are always foregrounded in Latin American literature. García Márquez discusses the crux of Latin America's solitude in his Nobel Lecture entitled 'The Solitude of Latin America':

> I dare to think that it is this outsized reality, and not just its literary expression, that has deserved the attention of the Swedish Academy of Letters. A reality not of paper, but one that lives within us and determines each instant of our countless daily deaths, and that nourishes a source of insatiable creativity, full of sorrow and beauty, of which this roving and nostalgic Colombian is but one cipher more, singled out by fortune. Poets and beggars, musicians and prophets, warriors and scoundrels, all creatures of that unbridled reality, we have had to ask but little of imagination, for our crucial problem has been a lack of conventional means to render our lives believable. This, my friends, is the crux of our solitude.[2]

The crux of the solitude of Latin America is not a lack of imagination, not a reality of paper, but a lack of and hence a need for 'conventional means to render our lives believable', a reality that lives inside them, determines their life and death and nourishes their source of creativity. What is desired is a life believable and a reality autonomous and creative. This lack of a believable life and a desire for such a life are revealed in the archive of *Chronicle of a Death Foretold*, whose reality full of coincidences and whose blurring of the demarcation between the fictional and the real, baffle not only the judge denied of even a fictitious proper name, but also the narrator and the reader. But the absence of a believable life only foregrounds the desire for such a life. García Márquez speaks of the utopia that Latin America pines for:

> … to oppression, plundering and abandonment, we respond with life. Neither floods nor plagues, nor famines nor cataclysms, nor even the eternal wars of century upon century have been able to subdue the persistent advantage of life over death. … Conversely, the most prosperous countries have succeeded in accumulating powers of destruction such as to annihilate, a hundred times over, not only all the human beings that have existed to this day but also the totality of all living beings that have ever drawn breath on this planet of misfortune.
>
> … Faced with this awesome reality that must have seemed a mere utopia through all of human time, we, the inventors of tales, who will believe anything, feel entitled to believe that it is not yet too late to engage in the creation of the opposite utopia. A new and sweeping utopia of life, where no one will be able to decide for others how they die, where love will prove true and happiness be possible, and where the races condemned to one hundred years of solitude will have, at last and forever, a second opportunity on earth. (Rosenberg 1992, 269)

The 'utopia' of the prosperous countries only causes what Peter Hulme calls 'colonial anxiety' (Hulme 1986, 1–2) experienced during the encounter between the colonizer and the colonized, and this anxiety creates an awesome reality for Latin America. But faced with such a grim and awesome reality of destruction, Latin America chooses to respond to it with life, to create an opposite utopia in

---

[2] pp. 267–8 in *Americas: An Anthology*, ed. by Mark B. Rosenberg, A. Douglas Kincaid and Kathleen Logan (New York and Oxford: Oxford University Press, 1992), Chapter 9.8, 'Gabriel García Márquez: Nobel Speech.' pp. 265–9.

which their life and death will be in their autonomy and their love and happiness will be true and possible. Only in such an opposite utopia, a utopia of life rather than the one of annihilation, whether cultural or physical, can there be a second opportunity on earth. These raiders' endeavour is to unsettle the colonial archive for a celebration of rebirth, for what Paz calls a renascence of life, an affirmation of creative energy, and a destabilization of the authority, which is a way to realize such a utopia of life.

The issue of the colonizing and patriarchal archive not only concerns Spain and Latin America, but also becomes global through the advent of advanced technology for archivization, like the computer and the Internet. The issue of the archive nowadays exceeds local specificity and becomes global. As Voss and Werner point out, the ideologically charged archive now becomes a 'windless region of hyperspace'.[3] This is what Rapaport refers to as the 'landless archive'.[4] New technology produces new modes of information, resulting in not only a new way of archivization, but also a new attitude towards life. The electronic archive offers new archival experience, and this new form of archive is getting more and more scholars' attention in various disciplines.[5] Kizza captures the importance of the Internet, saying that

> The Internet has resurrected the romantic myth of boundless space beyond the frontiers of known human civilization. New frontiers abound with infinite opportunities, where individuals can easily shed birth identities to acquire any identity of choice and where laws are self-made and observed (or broken) at will. (Kizza 1998, xi) (original bracketing)

Manuel Castells rightly points out that nowadays, the Internet somehow becomes an underlying structure of postmodern life,[6] offering a world of communication he calls 'the Internet Galaxy' (2001, 3). With the popularity of the computer, the Internet and the hyperspace, information turns into virtual and hard copies of manuscripts and documents go 'soft'. Such a seemingly limitless e-archive turns archival experience into an everyday event, and people get used to it so easily

---

[3] Paul J. Voss and Marta L. Werner, 'Toward a poetics of the archive: Introduction', in *Studies in the Literary Imagination*, Spring 1999; 32.1 (Atlanta: Georgia State University) p. i.

[4] Rapaport, *Later Derrida: Reading the Recent Work* p. 79. This is discussed in Chapter 4.

[5] See 'Archival action: the archive as ROM and its political instrumentalization under National Socialism' by Wolfgang Ernst, *History of the Human Sciences*, 1999, Vol. 12, No. 2, pp. 13–34 (London: SAGE Publications); 'Meno and the Internet: between memory and the archive' by Howard Caygill, *History of the Human Sciences*, 1999, Vol. 12, No. 2, pp. 1–11; 'The electronic archive' by George Myerson, *History of the Human Sciences*, 1998, Vol. 11, No. 4, pp. 85–101, to name just a few.

[6] Manuel Castells, *The Internet Galaxy: Reflections on the Internet, Business, and Society* (Oxford: Oxford University Press, 2001), p. 1. The phrase Castells uses is 'the Internet is the fabric of our lives'.

that they are not aware of accessing their own e-archive every day. A computer-user now becomes the archon of his own e-archive willy-nilly and creates his own 'software', like the 'joyceware' Derrida in 'Two Words for Joyce' discusses when the reader reads Joyce's works, for example, *Finnegans Wake* (Attridge and Ferrer 1984, 148). 'Each writing', according to Derrida, 'is at once the detached fragments of a software and a software more powerful than the other, a part larger than the whole of which it is a part' (Attridge and Ferrer 1984, 148). Each archive needs an archon, and now each computer-user becomes an archon of his own e-archive full of detailed fragments of a software. These fragments are larger than the software but at the same time part of it. However, Kizza points out the potential dangers of the Internet:

> The Internet medium consequently has given a new exposure to all sorts of human vices, giving them a new arena and, to some extent, a veiled degree of legitimacy. Such deeds have caught many civic groups, communities, regional groupings and governments off-guard, and many are struggling to come up with guidelines, policies and in some cases censorship mechanisms to regulate the Internet, which they see as getting out of control. (Kizza 1998, xii)

and Castells shares such a similar apprehension:

> the elasticity of the Internet makes it particularly susceptible to intensifying the contradictory trends present in our world[7]
>
> The Internet is indeed a technology of freedom – but it can free the powerful to oppress the uninformed, it may lead to the exclusion of the devalued by the conquerors of value. (Castells 2001, 275)

The Internet as e-archive has the essences of its ancestors, namely, preserving and reserving, protecting and patrolling, regulating and repressing. But all these are now done in a cyberspace.

George Myerson, when discussing other upsides and downsides of the e-archive, claims that the e-archive represents an endless chance of new insight and a synthesis of knowledge, which falls in line with the Western rationality of connecting and converging (Myerson 1998, 94). At the same time, the e-archive also symbolizes the 'glaciation of meaning', storing archival data which are frozen not flowing. What the e-archive offers is a future which is 'an era of unprecedented obliviousness, in which everything is recorded somewhere else' (Myerson 1998, 98). Worse still, the e-archive provides a virtual space in which everything is conserved, resulting in a 'cataloguable world' (Myerson 1998, 99)

---

7 Castells, *The Internet Galaxy*, p. 6. By 'elasticity', Castells refers to the appropriation and the potential uses and misuses of the Internet. The examples he quotes are the sectors of Colombian society 'appropriating the Internet for their own purposes, their criminal practices, rooted in a context of social injustice, political corruption, drug economy, and civil war' (p. 6).

where the archon of this e-archive can manipulate the data in whatever way he or she desires. In other words, the world is malleable and can be catalogued and classified according to the desire of the archon. Castells thinks likewise and says that

> the Internet is a particularly malleable technology, susceptible of being deeply modified by its social practice, and leading to a whole range of potential social outcomes. (Castells 2001, 5)

But the malleability of the Internet may not be easily attainable, since the data stored in the e-archive are simply too enormous to be manipulated or mastered. Hubert Dreyfus' study of artificial intelligence grows out of a sense of fear when facing the computer:

> Many people are torn between hopes and fears aroused by digital computers, which they find mostly incomprehensible and whose import therefore they cannot judge. (Dreyfus 1972, p. xi)

And Kizza points out other fears generated from the Internet, like the possibility of the individual personal identity being stolen, electronic surveillance and censorship (Kizza 1998, 52–62) and stresses the relationship between information overload and Information Fatigue Syndrome raised by Kathy Nellis (1997, 21):

> Second to information overload is individual health, what psychologists now refer to as Information Fatigue Syndrome. According to psychologist David Lewis, … "We're often seeing a failure of concentration. We are seeing a loss of motivation, loss of morale. We are seeing greater irritability." (Kizza 1998, 63–4)

This shows the helpless situation of the archon in his own e-archive, which is a situation in which the excessive information creates a sense of fatigue, a state of incomprehension, a place to get lost. This is what Borges allegorizes in 'The Library of Babel' and 'Funes the Memorious'.

In such an archive in the new technological age, it is by no means easy to distinguish true information from the false one, or to access, read and master each hypertext. This is a virtual space without trace. Benjamin in *Charles Baudelaire* says 'living means leaving traces' (Benjamin 1973, 169). But living in such a cyberspace and in his own e-archive, the archon can never leave any trace. Even trace turns virtual. The e-archive seems to be able to guarantee a more 'permanent' storage of information, but actually it can be a 'garbage heap' like Funes' memory, if generalization of the data fails. At the same time, data stored in this archive in fact are threatened by new sources of oblivion – power-cut and computer virus. Maybe, one way of mastering it or of living with it is to be playful not only with the benefits it offers, but also with the drawbacks and dangers it entails.

When the e-archive on the Internet is surfed or cruised, Mark Nunes points out that this cyberspace for computer-mediated communication actually offers two figurations of virtual topography, namely a linear, pointed-oriented and Cartesian, and one a fluid, plane-oriented and unbounded one. He likens the former one to what Deleuze and Guattari call the 'striated space', and the latter one to the 'smooth space'.[8] In this cyberspace, 'the striated "highway" topography determines cyberspace as a system of regulated connections between determined points on dedicated lines; conversely, a smooth "plane" topography "writes" a cyberspace of fluid transit and continual passage' (Nunes 1999, 62). Mark Nunes says that these are two spatial arrangements with two systems – the former being State-oriented and static, following a gravitational principle and having a totalitarian structure, while the latter being nomadic and fluid, providing a space of de-territorialization and offering users infinite degrees of freedom (Nunes 1999, 63–4). Both the striated space and the smooth space on the Internet in fact can be regarded as the co-existence of the e-archive and the hypertext. The e-archive is like its ancestor – patriarchal, originating and totalizing in nature, while the hypertext is like the manuscript – liberating, non-totalizable and non-attributable.

These two topographies – the e-archive and the hypertext, or the striated space and the smooth space, can be found in each other in this cyberspace, as Mark Nunes points out – 'the smooth irrupting in the striated, the striated capturing the smooth'. He is positive about this, believing that 'this mixing provides crossings for both systems that keep cyberspace always "virtual," always in the act of becoming: real, yet never completely determined' (Nunes 1999, 74). Steven Shaviro says that this cyberspace can be regarded as a realization of Foucault's heterotopias – metastable and dynamic 'otherspaces, or space of otherness' formed by 'shifting subjectivities' and 'nomadic displacements'.[9] It may be true that in the limitless cyberspace, which allows unbounded hypertexts, the essences of the (e-)archive – patriarchal, totalizing and originating – sink into oblivion. But the complexity of the Internet as e-archive should not be overlooked, especially when the process of globalization is in full swing. The Internet allows instantaneous 'global transmission of signs and symbols', which characterizes contemporary society and thus entails a 'continuous global flow of ideas, information, commitment, values and tastes' (Dash 1998, 52), but at the same time, this globalization can be understood as a 'homogenizing process of Westernization, cultural imperialism, and mass consumerism' (Dash 1998, 52).[10] In the context of globalization, it is doubtful whether the Internet and the e-archive can be a liberating heterotopia.

---

[8] Mark Nunes, 'Virtual Topographies: Smooth and Striated Cyberspace' in *Cyberspace Textuality: Computer Technology and Literary Theory*, ed. Marie-Laure Ryan, (Bloomington: Indiana University Press, 1999), p. 62. For the discussion on the striated space and the smooth space, see Deleuze and Guattari's *A Thousand Plateaus: Capitalism and Schizophrenia*, trans. Brian Massumi (Minneapolis and London: University of Minnesota Press, 1987), Chapter 14, '1440: The Smooth and the Striated.'

[9] Steven Shaviro, "13.Pavel Curtis," *Doom Patrols*, 1995. http://dhalgren.english.washington.edu/~steve/ch13.html.

[10] See also Malcolm Waters' *Globalization* (London and New York: Routledge, 1995), pp. 125–6; and Leo Ching's 'Globalizing the Regional, Regionalizing the Global: Mass Culture and Asianism in the Age of Late Capital' in *Globalization*, ed. Arjun Appadurai (Durham, NC and London: Duke University Press, 2001), p. 295.

The Internet as a huge e-archive creates fantasy. The archon of such an e-archive becomes more and more like Philip II, who dreams of building his empire held together by manuscripts and archives, and who has a strong desire to accumulate and manipulate information. But this e-archive fails to be totalizing or homogenizing because of the immense quantity of data. This is the Library of Babel in the age of electronic technology. The e-archive now becomes a non-attributable, non-originating virtual space. In this regard, it is as liberating and non-totalizable as a feminine manuscript. However, it can be patriarchal in terms of globalization, being homogenizing on a global scale. It may be that the e-archive, together with hypertexts, constructs a new space for the reader and the storyteller – an androgynous space in which the essences of both the archive and the manuscript amalgamate. If so, intriguing issues arise, like the possibility of story-telling in such a virtual space, the difference of the way one reads or writes in such an e-archive from the past, and how such an androgynous e-archive can be raided. The archive, whether it is the traditional one or the electronic one, remains a fascinating topic.

Bibliography

Almodóvar, Pedro (dir. and screenplay) *Talk to Her (Hable con Ella)*, perf. Javier Camara, Leonor Watling, Dario Grandinetti, Rosario Flores (Sony Pictures, 2002).

Appadurai, Arjun (ed.), *Globalization* (Durham, NC and London: Duke University Press, 2001).

Arabian Nights' Entertainments, ed. Robert L. Mack (Oxford: Oxford University Press, 1995).

The Arabian Nights: Tales from A Thousand and One Nights, trans. Richard F. Burton (New York: The Modern Library, 2001).

Attridge, Derek and Daniel Ferrer (eds.), *Post-structural Joyce: Essays from the French* (Cambridge: Cambridge University Press, 1984).

Auerbach, Erich, *Mimesis: The Representation of Reality in Western Literature*, trans. Willard R. Trask (Princeton, NJ: Princeton University Press, 1953).

Bacarisse, Pamela, *The Necessary Dream: A Study of the Novels of Manuel Puig* (Totowa, NJ: Barnes and Noble Books, 1988).

Bakhtin, Mikhail, *Rabelais and His World*, trans. Helene Iswolsky (Bloomington and Indianapolis: Indiana University Press, 1984).

———, *Problems of Dostoevsky's Poetics*, ed. and trans. Caryl Emerson (Minneapolis: University of Minnesota Press, 1984).

Bataille, Georges, *Visions of Excess: Selected Writings, 1927–1939*, trans. Allan Stoekl (Minneapolis: University of Minnesota Press, 1985).

Bell-Villada, Gene H., *García Márquez: The Man and His Work* (Chapel Hill and London: The University of North Carolina Press, 1990).

———, *Borges and His Fiction: A Guide to His Mind and Art* (Austin: University of Texas Press, 1999).

Benjamin, Walter, *Charles Baudelaire* (London and New York: Verso, 1973).

———, *The Origin of German Tragic Drama*, trans. John Osborne (London: Verso, 1998).

The Bible, Authorized King James Version with Apocrypha (Oxford: Oxford University Press, 1998).

Bloom, Harold (ed.), *Gabriel García Márquez* (New York: Chelsea House Publisher, 1989).

Bondanella, Peter, *Umberto Eco and the open text: Semiotics, fiction, popular culture* (Cambridge: Cambridge University Press, 1997).

Borges, Jorge Luis, *Labyrinths*, trans. James E. Irby (Harmondsworth: Penguin Books, 1964).

———, *Jorge Luis Borges: Collected Fictions*, trans. Andrew Hurley (Harmondsworth: Penguin Books, 1998).

———, *Selected Poems*, ed. Alexander Coleman (Harmondsworth: Penguin Books, 2000).

———, *The Total Library: Non-Fiction 1922–1986*, trans. Esther Allen, Suzanne Jill Levine and Eliot Weinberger (Harmondsworth: Penguin Books, 1999).

Browne, Ray B. and Lawrence A. Kreiser, Jr., *The Detective as Historian: History and Art in Historical Crime Fiction* (Bowling Green, OH: Bowling Green State University Popular Press, 2000).

Capozzi, Rocco, *Reading Eco: An Anthology* (Bloomington and Indianapolis: Indiana University Press, 1997).

Castells, Manuel, *The Internet Galaxy: Reflections on the Internet, Business, and Society* (Oxford: Oxford University Press, 2001).

Caviglia, John, 'The Tales of Borges: Language and the Private Eye', *MLN*, Vol. 89, No. 2, Hispanic Issue (March 1974), pp. 219–31 (Baltimore: The Johns Hopkins University Press, 1974).

Caygill, Howard, 'Meno and the Internet: between memory and the archive', *History of the Human Sciences*, Vol. 12, No. 2, pp. 1–11 (London: SAGE Publications, 1999).

de Cervantes Saavedra, Miguel, *Don Quixote de la Mancha*, trans. Charles Jarvis (New York: Oxford University Press, 1992).

———, *The Ingenious Hidalgo Don Quixote de la Mancha*, trans. John Rutherford (Harmondsworth: Penguin Books, 2001).

———, *The History and Adventures of the Renowned Don Quixote*, trans. Tobias Smollett (New York: The Modern Library, 2001).

———, *Don Quixote*, trans. Edith Grossman (New York: HarperCollins, 2003).

———, *Exemplary Stories*, trans. Lesley Lipson (Oxford: Oxford University Press, 1998).

Christie, John S., 'Fathers and Virgins: García Márquez's Faulknerian *Chronicle of a Death Foretold*', *Latin American Literary Review*, Vol. XXI, No. 41, January–June 1993, pp. 21–9 (Pittsburgh: University of Pittsburgh, 1993).

Close, Anthony, *The Romantic Approach to 'Don Quixote': A Critical History of the Romantic Tradition in 'Quixote' Criticism* (Cambridge: Cambridge University Press, 1977).

Copleston, Frederick Charles, *A History of Philosophy Vol. 1: Greece and Rome* (New York: Image Books, 1993).

Corominas, Joan, *Breve diccionario etimológico de la lengua castellana.* (Madrid: Gredos, 1961).

de Costa, Elena M., *Latin American Literary Review*, Vol. XI, Fall–Winter 1982, No. 21, pp. 63–7 (Pittsburgh: University of Pittsburgh, 1982).

Coward, Harold and Toby Foshay (eds.), *Derrida and Negative Theology* (Albany: State University of New York, 1992).

Curtius, Ernst Robert, *Europe Literature and the Latin Middle Ages*, trans. Willard R. Trask (Princeton, NJ: Princeton University Press, 1983).

Dante Alighieri, *The Divine Comedy Vol. I: Inferno*, trans. Mark Musa (Harmondsworth: Penguin Books, 1984).

———, *The Divine Comedy Vol. III: Paradise*, trans. Mark Musa (Harmondsworth: Penguin Books, 1986).

Dash, Robert C., 'Globalization: For Whom and for What', *Latin American Perspectives*, Issue 103, Vol. 25, No. 6, pp. 52–4, November 1998 (Thousand Oaks, CA: Sage Publications, 1998).

Deleuze, Gilles and Felix Guattari, *A Thousand Plateaus: Capitalism and Schizophrenia*, trans. Brian Massumi (Minneapolis and London: University of Minnesota Press, 1987).

Derrida, Jacques, *Writing and Difference*, trans. Alan Bass (Chicago: The University of Chicago Press, 1978).

———, *Spurs: Nietzsche's Styles*, trans. Barbara Harlow (Chicago and London: The University of Chicago Press, 1978).

———, *Margins of Philosophy*, trans. Alan Bass (Chicago: The University of Chicago Press, 1982).

———, *Cinders*, trans. Ned Lukacher (Lincoln: University of Nebraska Press, 1991).

———, *Acts of Literature*, ed. Derek Attridge (New York and London: Routledge, 1992).

———, *Points ... Interviews, 1974–1994*, ed. Elisabeth Weber, trans. by Peggy Kamuf et al. (Palo Alto, CA: Stanford University Press, 1995).

———, *Archive Fever: A Freudian Impression*, trans. Eric Prenowitz (Chicago and London: The University of Chicago Press, 1996).

Dickens, Charles, *The Posthumous Papers of the Pickwick Club* (Harmondsworth: Penguin Books, 1999).

Dreyfus, Hubert L., *What Computers Can't Do: A Critique of Artificial Reason* (New York: Harper and Row Publishers, 1972).

Echevarría, Roberto González, *Myth and Archive: A Theory of Latin American Narrative* (Durham, NC and London: Duke University Press, 1998).

Eco, Umberto, *Postscript to The Name of the Rose*, trans. William Weaver (San Diego: Harcourt Brace Jovanovich Inc, 1984).

———, *The Name of the Rose*, trans. William Weaver (London: Minerva, 1992).

Elliott, John Huxtable, *Imperial Spain, 1469–1716* (London: Edward Arnold (Publishers) Ltd., 1963).

———, *Spain and its World, 1500–1700* (New Haven and London: Yale University Press, 1989).

Ernst, Wolfgang, 'Archival action: the archive as ROM and its political instrumentalization under National Socialism', *History of the Human Sciences*, Vol. 12, No. 2, pp. 13–34 (London: SAGE Publications, 1999).

Finch, Patricia S., 'Rojas' Celestina and Cervantes' Cañizares', *Cervantes: Bulletin of the Cervantes Society of America*, Vol. 9, No. 2 (Gainesville, FL: the Society, 1989).

Fletcher, Angus, *Allegory: The Theory of a Symbolic Mode* (Ithaca and London: Cornell University Press, 1964).

Forcione, Alban K., *Cervantes and the Mystery of Lawlessness: A Study of El casamiento engañoso y El coloquio de los perros* (Princeton, NJ: Princeton University Press, 1984).

Foucault, Michel, *The Archaeology of Knowledge and The Discourse on Language*, trans. A.M. Sheridan Smith (New York: Pantheon Books, 1972).

———, *Language, Counter-memory, Practice: Selected Essays and Interviews*, trans. Donald F. Bouchard and Sherry Simon (Ithaca, New York: Cornell University Press, 1977).

———, 'Of Other Spaces', in *Diacritics*, Spring 1986 (Ithaca, NY: Cornell University, 1986).

Freud, Sigmund, 'The Uncanny', in *The Standard Edition of The Complete Psychological Works of Sigmund Freud, Vol. XVII (1917–1919): An Infantile Neurosis and Other Works*, trans. James Strachey (London: Vintage, 1955).

———, *The Interpretation of Dreams, The Penguin Freud Library Vol. 4*, trans. and ed. James Strachey (Harmondsworth: Penguin, 1976).

———, 'From the History of an Infantile Neurosis (The 'Wolf Man')', *The Penguin Freud Library Vol. 9: Case Histories II*, trans. James Strachey (Harmondsworth: Penguin Books, 1979).

Genette, Gérard, *Narrative Discourse: An Essay in Method*, trans. Jane E. Lewin (New York: Cornell University Press, 1980).

Haft, Adele., Jane White and Robert White, *The Key to "The Name of the Rose"* (Ann Arbor: The University of Michigan Press, 1999).

Hansen, Terence L., 'Folk Narrative Motifs, Beliefs, and Proverbs in Cervantes' *Exemplary Novels', The Journal of American Folklore*, Vol. 72, No. 283 (January–March 1959), pp. 24–9 (Arlington: American Folklore Society, 1959).

Hart, Thomas, R., 'Cervantes's Sententious Dogs', *MLN*, Vol. 94, No. 2, Hispanic Issue (March 1979), pp. 377–86 (Baltimore: The Johns Hopkins University Press, 1979).

———, 'Renaissance Dialogue Into Novel: Cervantes's Coloquio', *MLN*, Vol. 105, No. 2, Hispanic Issue (March 1990), pp. 191–202 (Baltimore: The Johns Hopkins University Press, 1990).

Homer, *The Odyssey*, trans. Robert Fagles (Harmondsworth: Penguin Books, 1996).

Hulme, Peter, *Colonial Encounters: Europe and the native Caribbean, 1492–1797* (London and New York: Methuen, 1986).

James, Henry, *The Aspern Papers and The Turn of the Screw* (Harmondsworth: Penguin Books, 1984).

Johnson, Carroll, *Madness and Lust: A Psychoanalytical Approach to " Don Quixote"* (Berkeley: University of California Press, 1983).

Joyce, James, *Finnegans Wake* (Harmondsworth: Penguin Books, 1992).

Keats, John, *Complete Poems*, ed. Jack Stillinger (Cambridge, MA: The Belknap Press of Harvard University Press, 1982).

Kerr, Lucille, *Suspended Fictions: Reading Novels by Manuel Puig* (Urbana and Chicago: University of Illinois Press, 1987).

Kizza, Joséph Migga, *Civilizing the Internet: Global Concerns and Efforts Toward Regulation* (Jefferson, North Carolina, and London: McFarland and Company Inc. Publishers, 1998).

Kristeva, Julia, *Desire in Language: A Semiotic Approach to Literature and Art*, trans. Thomas Gora, Alice Jardine and Leon S. Roudiez (New York: Columbia University Press, 1980).

Lacan, Jacques, *Écrits: A Selection*, trans. Alan Sheridan (New York and London: W. W. Norton and Co., 1977).

Laplanche, J. and J.-B. Pontalis, *The Language of Psycho-Analysis*, trans. Donald Nicholson-Smith (New York and London: W.W. Norton and Co., 1973).

Lavine, T.Z., *From Socrates to Sartre: the Philosophic Quest* (New York: Bantam Books, 1984).

Lewis, Daniel K., *History of Argentina* (Westport: Greenwood Press, 2001).

Lyotard, Jean-François, *The Inhuman: Reflections on Time* (Palo Alto, CA: Stanford University Press, 1991).

de Madariaga, Salvador, *Don Quixote: An introductory essay in psychology* (London: Geoffrey Cumberledge, 1948).

McGuirk, Bernard and Richard Cardwell (eds.), *Gabriel García Márquez: New Readings* (Cambridge: Cambridge University Press, 1987).

McMurray, George R. (ed.), *Critical Essays on Gabriel García Márquez* (Boston: G.K. Hall and Co, 1987).

de Man, Paul, *Blindness and Insight: Essays in the Rhetoric of Contemporary Criticism*, 2nd ed. (Minneapolis: University of Minnesota Press, 1983).

Mancing, Howard, *The Chivalric World of Don Quijote: Style, Structure, and Narrative Technique* (Columbia: University of Missouri Press, 1982).

Manoff, Marlene, 'Theories of the Archive from Across the Disciplines', in *Portal: Libraries and the Academy*, Vol. 4, No. 1, pp. 9–25 (Baltimore: The Johns Hopkins University Press, 2004).

Maravall, José Antonio, *Utopia and Counterutopia in the "Quixote"*, trans. Robert W. Felkel (Detroit: Wayne State University Press, 1991).

Márquez, Gabriel García, *Chronicle of a Death Foretold*, trans. Gregory Rabassa (Harmondsworth: Penguin Books, 1982).

———, *One Hundred Years of Solitude*, trans. Gregory Rabassa (New York: Perennial Classics, 1998).

Martin, Gerald, *Journeys through the Labyrinth: Latin American Fiction in the Twentieth Century* (London: Verso, 1989).

Martín, Jorge Hernández, *Readers and Labyrinths: Detective Fiction in Borges, Bustos Domecq and Eco* (New York and London: Garland Publishing, Inc., 1995).

Miller, J. Hillis, *The Linguistic Moment: From Wordsworth to Stevens* (Princeton, NJ: Princeton University Press, 1985).

Myerson, George, 'The electronic archive', *History of the Human Sciences*, Vol. 11, No. 4, pp. 85–101 (London: SAGE Publications, 1998).

Nellis, Kathy, 'Expert Information Onslaught Bad for Your Health', *CNN-Interactive*, April 15, 1997. Also at http://cnn.com/Tech9704/information.overload/.

Nietzsche, Friedrich, *The Gay Science*, trans. Walter Kaufmann (New York: Vintage Books, 1974).

———, *On the Genealogy of Morals*, trans. Walter Kaufmann (New York: Vintage Books, 1989).

———, *Untimely Meditations*, ed. Daniel Breazeale, trans. R.J. Hollingdale (Cambridge: Cambridge University Press, 1997).

Olster, Stacey, *The Trash Phenomenon: Contemporary Literature, Popular Culture, and the Making of the American Century* (Athens and London: The University of Georgia Press, 2003).

Ortega, Julio (ed.), *Gabriel García Márquez and the Powers of Fiction* (Austin: University of Texas Press, 1988).

Panofsky, Erwin, *The Life and Art of Albrecht Dürer* (Princeton, NJ: Princeton University Press, 1955).

Parker, Allene M., 'Drawing Borges: A Two-Part Invention on the Labyrinths of Jorge Luis Borges and M.C. Escher', *Rocky Mountain Review of Language and Literature*, Vol. 55, No. 2, pp. 11–23 (Salt Lake City: Rocky Mountain Modern Language Association, 2001).

Pavel, Thomas, 'The Borders of Fiction', *Poetics Today*, Vol. 4, No. 1, pp. 83–8 (Durham, NC: Duke University, 1983).

Paz, Octavio, *The Labyrinth of Solitude and Other Writings*, trans. Lysander Kemp, Yara Milos and Rachel Phillips Belash (New York: Grove Press, 1985).

Penuel, Arnold M., *Intertextuality in García Márquez* (Rock Hill, SC: Spanish Literature Publications Company, 1994).

Plato, *The Republic*, trans. Desmond Lee, 2nd edition (Harmondsworth: Penguin Books, 1974).

Poe, Edgar Allan, *The Fall of the House of Usher and Other Writings* (Harmondsworth: Penguin Books, 1986).

Propp, Vladimir, *Morphology of the Folktale*, trans. Laurence Scott (Austin: University of Texas Press, 1968).

Puig, Manuel, *Kiss of the Spider Woman*, trans. Thomas Colchie (New York: Vintage Books, 1979).

Purkiss, Diane, *The Witch in History: Early Modern and Twentieth-century Representations* (London and New York: Routledge, 1996).

Rapaport, Herman, *Later Derrida: Reading the Recent Work* (New York and London: Routledge, 2003).

Rock, David, *Authoritarian Argentina: The Nationalist Movement, Its History and Its Impact* (Berkeley: University of California Press, 1993).

de Rojas, Fernando, *Celestina*, trans. James Mabbe (Warminster: Aris and Phillips Ltd., 1987).

Rosenberg, Mark B., A. Douglas Kincaid and Kathleen Logan (eds.), *Americas: An Anthology* (New York and Oxford: Oxford University Press, 1992).

Ryan, Marie-Laure (ed.), *Cyberspace Textuality: Computer Technology and Literary Theory* (Bloomington: Indiana University Press, 1999).

Saffar, Ruth Anthony El and Diana de Armas Wilson (eds.), *Quixotic Desire: Psychoanalytic Perspectives on Cervantes* (Ithaca, New York: Cornell University Press, 1993).

Shakespeare, William, *Troilus and Cressida*, ed. Kenneth Palmer (The Arden Shakespeare) (London: Routledge, 1989).

Shaviro, Steven, '13.Pavel Curtis', *Doom Patrols*, 1995. http://dhalgren.english.washington.edu/~steve/ch13.html.

Southworth, Herbert R., *Conspiracy and the Spanish War: the brainwashing of Francisco Franco* (London: Routledge, 2002).

Sullivan, Henry W., *Grotesque Purgatory: A Study of Cervantes's Don Quixote, Part II* (University Park,: The Pennsylvania State University Press, 1996).

Swanson, Philip, *The new novel in Latin America: Politics and popular culture after the Boom* (Manchester and New York: Manchester University Press, 1995).

Tales from the Thousand and One Nights, trans. N.J. Dawood (Harmondsworth: Penguin Books, 1973).

Tambling, Jeremy, *Narrative and Ideology* (Milton Keynes and Philadelphia: Open University Press, 1991).

Thiem, Jon, 'The Great Library of Alexandria Burnt: Towards the History of a Symbol', *Journal of the History of Ideas*, Vol. 40, No. 4 (October–December 1979), pp. 507–26 (Baltimore: The Johns Hopkins University Press, 1979).

———, 'Borges, Dantes and the Poetics of Total Vision', *Comparative Literature*, Vol. 40, No. 2 (Spring 1988), pp. 97–121 (Eugene: University of Oregon, 1988).

Thomas, Keith, *Religion and the Decline of Magic* (New York: Scribner's Sons, 1971).

Tittler, Jonathan, *Manuel Puig* (New York: Twayne Publishers, 1993).

Todorov, Tzvetan, *The Poetics of Prose*, trans. Richard Howard (Ithaca, New York: Cornell University Press, 1977).

Tuchman, Barbara, *A Distant Mirror: The Calamitous 14th Century* (Harmondsworth: Penguin, 1979).

Virgil (Publius Vergilius Maro), *The Aeneid*, trans. Jackson Knight (Harmondsworth: Penguin Books, 1958).

Voss, Paul J. and Marta L. Werner, 'Toward a poetics of the archive: Introduction', in *Studies in the Literary Imagination*, Spring 1999; 32.1, pp. i–viii (Atlanta: Georgia State University, 1999).

Waters, Malcolm, *Globalization* (London and New York: Routledge, 1995).

Williamson, Edwin (ed.), *Cervantes and the Modernists: The Question of Influence* (London: Tamesis Books Ltd, 1994).

Wilson, Diana de Armas, '"Passing the Love of Women": The Intertextuality of *El curioso impertinente', Cervantes: Bulletin of the Cervantes Society of America*, Vol. 7, No. 2 (Gainesville: the Society, 1987).

Wordsworth, William, *The Prelude, 1799, 1805, 1850*, ed. Jonathan Wordsworth, M.H. Abrams, and Stephen Gill (New York: W.W. Norton and Company, 1979).

Index

For Product Safety Concerns and Information please contact our EU representative GPSR@taylorandfrancis.com
Taylor & Francis Verlag GmbH, Kaufingerstraße 24, 80331 München, Germany

www.ingramcontent.com/pod-product-compliance
Lightning Source LLC
Chambersburg PA
CBHW060528310726
48982CB00002B/470

* 9 7 8 0 7 5 4 6 6 5 3 3 5 *